TALKING TO HEAVEN

TALKING TO HEAVEN

A MEDIUM'S MESSAGE
OF LIFE AFTER DEATH

JAMES VAN PRAAGH

A DUTTON BOOK

DUTTON
Published by the Penguin Group
Penguin Putnam Inc., 375 Hudson Street, New York, New York 10014, U.S.A.
Penguin Books Ltd, 27 Wrights Lane, London W8 5TZ, England
Penguin Books Australia Ltd, Ringwood, Victoria, Australia
Penguin Books Canada Ltd, 10 Alcorn Avenue, Toronto, Ontario, Canada M4V 3B2
Penguin Books (N.Z.) Ltd, 182–190 Wairau Road, Auckland 10, New Zealand

Penguin Books Ltd, Registered Offices:
Harmondsworth, Middlesex, England

First published by Dutton, an imprint of Dutton Signet,
a member of Penguin Putnam Inc.

First Printing, November, 1997
11 13 15 17 19 20 18 16 14 12

 REGISTERED TRADEMARK—MARCA REGISTRADA

LIBRARY OF CONGRESS CATALOGING-IN-PUBLICATION DATA:
Van Praagh, James.
Talking to heaven : a medium's message of life after death / James Van Praagh.
p. cm.
Includes bibliographical references.
ISBN 0-525-94268-8 (alk. paper)
1. Van Praagh, James. 2. Mediums—United States—Biography. 3. Spiritualism.
I. Title.
BF1283.V29A3   1997
133.9'1—dc21   97-24861
CIP

Printed in the United States of America
Set in Garamond
Designed by Jesse Cohen

The individual experiences recounted in this book are true. However, in some instances, names and other descriptive details have been altered to protect the identities of the people involved.

This book is printed on acid-free paper.

To Connie,
The very first angel I met on earth,
who showed me how to catch the sun.

CONTENTS

ACKNOWLEDGMENTS

When one begins the task of chronologically recalling personal experiences by breathing life into words, it is done with the hope that, in some small way, these expressions will create a sense of knowledge and wonder as well as aid in the enlightenment of another's path. Writing this book was an undertaking that could not possibly have been executed alone. It was created by the blending of thoughts, ideas, experiences and lives of those who have dearly touched me.

I first must give appreciation to the "Creative Expression" identified under various titles such as God, Allah, Yahweh, Divine Being, and The Great Light. I will just refer to this Power as the "Source," the Source of All.

I would like to acknowledge those beloved souls on this earth's plane who have come to me with stories of both tragedy and love, seeking guidance, closure, healing, and peace. I hope I have fulfilled their expectations and have been able to place their minds and hearts to rest.

I thank and appreciate all those dear ones in the spirit world, who like dreams come back through me to relay earthly experiences to their families and friends. These remembrances, now woven into the tapestry of time, will provide evidence and comfort, proving that there is no death, only life. Through the power of love and only love, these heart-strung spirits align themselves with us, providing courage, strength, power, and guidance, and assisting us in fulfilling our individual earthly destinies.

I want to thank my heavenly guides and teachers who have been with me from the initial birth of my gift. They have never failed to incorporate their strength, power, and wisdom into my work, displaying an example for growth, illumination, and upliftment, not only for self but for all humankind.

I also give my love and gratitude to those on this earth plane who have assisted me along the path with their love, encouragement, and support: Brian E. Hurst, Carol Shoemaker, Mary Ann Saxon, Marilyn Jensen, Peter Redgrove, Linda Tomchin, and Cammy Farone.

To all my family, friends, and loves of this lifetime, I live in gratitude to each and every one of you. For the time we share together on this earth has not only enriched my soul but has taught me valuable lessons in the emotional expression of the human heart. Love celebrates life. I thank you for celebrating the fullness of what we were, what we are, and what we are yet to become.

To all, thank you for sharing your light and sharing this neverending journey of love and life hand-in-hand.

·SECTION ONE·

THE UNVEILING

CHAPTER 1

The Medium

I am often asked if I was born a medium or if I was transformed into one by a terrible illness, or a freak accident that caused some sort of head trauma, or a near-death experience. As hair-raising as those possibilities may be, I cannot claim any one of them as the dramatic moment that introduced me to my life's work.

I am not unlike anyone else. We are all born with some level of psychic ability. The question is: Do we recognize our psychic abilities and act upon them? Like many others, I didn't know what it meant to have psychic ability. It was probably on some TV game show that I first heard the term "psychic." I was lucky enough to pronounce it, let alone understand its definition. It was a word that came closest to explaining why I *knew* things about people when they walked into a room. It was also the reason my first-grade Catholic school teacher kept me after school one day.

Lunch break was over, and all the kids were heading back to the classroom. I had just put away my Yogi Bear lunch box when my teacher, Mrs. Weinlick, walked into the room. Our eyes met, and a feeling of sadness instantly came over me. Then I walked up to her and said, "Everything is going to be all right. John broke his leg." She looked at me with a cross expression and said, "What are you talking about?" I replied, "John was hit by a car, but he is okay. He just broke his leg." Well, I thought her eyes were going to pop straight out of her head. She pointed to my seat and told me to sit in it for the rest of the day. About an hour later, the principal came to the door and spoke with Mrs. Weinlick. Suddenly, Mrs. Weinlick panicked, turned white, and ran out of the room screaming.

The next day Mrs. Weinlick seemed to be back to her normal self, except that she did not stop staring at me the whole day. She asked me to stay after school so she could talk to me. God bless her! It was her talk that introduced me to my psychic ability. It seemed that on the previous day, her son John was hit by a car, but, miraculously, he had just broken his leg. She asked me: "How did you know it was going to happen?" I didn't know how to answer her. I just knew it. I had a sense about it. She stared at me, and I started to cry. *Was I responsible for creating this accident and maiming her son?*

Well, needless to say, she calmed me down and told me not to get upset. "Many children and grown-up people know things before they happen," noted Mrs. Weinlick. She said that I was "one of God's messengers" and that God had given me a special gift. She continued, "So that one day you could help people." She told me not to ever feel bad about things I might see in my mind. "You are special," she said. But she warned me to be careful with whom I share my *specialness*.

That was my first explanation of psychic ability. When I look back on that time, I am grateful to Mrs. Weinlick for explaining it to me. It was an aid to me in so many ways. If I had had a nun for my homeroom teacher instead of a layperson, my life might have turned out a lot differently.

Today, I fully understand my ability to see and feel things that are not of this physical world. Often referred to as a *sixth sense*, psychic ability is also known as intuition, gut feeling, a hunch, or a certain *knowingness* one has about something. And all of us use this ability every day without even knowing it. For instance, how many times have you thought of someone, and minutes later the phone rings and that person is on the other end of the line? Or you get a hunch to switch lanes in traffic, and you find out further along the way that there was an accident in the other lane. Perhaps you get a feeling on the way to work that the boss is going to be in a bad mood, and sure enough you get to work and it's true. How many times have you been thinking of a song, and minutes later you hear it on the radio? These are all examples of psychic ability. Where does this sixth sense come from? In Greek, the word *psychic* means "of the soul." When we use our psychic ability, we are tuning into the energy of the soul, or the natural life force that permeates every living creature.

As infants, we are even more psychic than we are as adults—maybe not more psychic but more open to our psychic senses. Not only because we are still very close to the other side of life but also because our speech and thoughts are not developed so we have to rely on our feelings, or our sensing, to relate to the physical world. We have all seen a baby start to cry when held by one person and stop immediately when held by another. The baby surely senses a more harmonious or safer vibration with the second individual. That is why babies always want their mothers. A strong psychic link exists between a mother and her baby. How often will a mother run into the baby's room knowing she is needed just as her baby wakes up? This link continues to grow stronger and stronger, and soon a mother just senses her baby's needs without any verbal signals from the child at all.

Psychic energy is also at work in the plant and animal kingdoms. Plants are extremely sensitive and often thrive very nicely when they sense a gentle and friendly environment in which they are cared for and feel loved. This reminds me of a very interesting story. When I was working a regular nine-to-five job, I drove a coworker home one day. As I sat in her apartment, I heard a very high-pitched sound. This screaming vibration was all around me. It was as if someone was hurt and crying for help. I looked around and finally realized what it was. All of the plants in her apartment were dried up and dying. They were screaming for water. I immediately told the woman, and she informed me that she hadn't watered them for over two weeks.

The idea of plants screaming might seem strange to many. To those, I suggest reading books on the subject, especially one called *The Secret Life of Plants* by Peter Tomkins. We must realize that the magic of LIFE comes in all forms, shapes, and sizes, even plants. We can learn more about these life-forms if we take the time to listen and open up to our own psychic ability and to the energies all around us.

Besides the plant kingdom, animals are known to rely on a sixth sense. Witness the behavior of your own Fido or Kitty. How often have you seen a dog cower or bark relentlessly when it meets a certain individual? Or how it tends to stick around one person more than another while roaming around a room full of people. Or, during natural disasters, such as earthquakes, tornadoes, or hurricanes, an animal tends to become restless and disoriented, and often hides in a closet or underneath furniture. The animal is not getting the news from the TV set like us. It just knows. Usually animals sense a disaster before it strikes. They are highly sensitive to human anxiety as well. If you want to know a weather forecast, observe the nearby cattle. Before a storm, cows can often be found lying down on the grass. Throughout creation, animals have depended on their psychic sense or instinct to assist them in protecting themselves and sustaining life.

I Want to See God for Myself

Even before I thought about my psychic ability, I used to think a lot about the existence of God. Although I was raised Catholic and attended nine years of Catholic school, I found the Catholic view of God to be too limited and unrealistic. We had to believe in a deity on blind faith, and that confused me all the more. I was plagued with questions like: *How do we know God really exists? Has anyone ever seen God? How does God make things from nothing? Who wrote the stories in the Bible, and are they true?*

As much as I wanted to believe in the God molded by the rituals and laws of the Church, I did not feel a personal experience of God inside me. *Was it my duty simply to live out this daily ceremony?* I felt I was missing a piece of the puzzle. *Had the nuns kept something from me? Did I miss something at mass that everyone else had picked up on? Was I the only one to question their beliefs?* The request seemed simple enough in my young mind: *If there is a God, please show me proof.*

My prayer was answered when I was eight years old. I was lying in bed early one morning when I felt a strong gust of cold wind blow across my face. I pulled the blankets closer to me and looked over to my bedroom window. It was tightly shut. As I tried to figure out how that gust of wind got in my room, I looked up and saw a large hand, palm down, coming from the ceiling. The hand glowed with a pulsating white light. I was mesmerized, but somehow unafraid. I didn't understand what was happening, but perhaps because I was a child, I had no fear. I was willing to accept the image I was seeing as real. I was suddenly filled with an overwhelming sense of peace, love, and joy. Although there was no booming voice of God (as often described in the Bible) to answer my questions or reveal my destiny, I knew that this vision was God. I also knew that I would do whatever was necessary to experience that joyful feeling again. I began to understand that there was much more to life than what I had been taught and what I could see through my physical eyes.

The illuminated hand of God was my first clairvoyant experience, and though the impact was impressive, I never mentioned it to anyone. I felt it was my secret and that no one would believe me anyway. Later, I would learn much more about clairvoyance, when the mind is impressed with various images, shapes, scenes, spirits, faces, and remote locations not visible to the physical eye. For example, before falling asleep at night, a number of different forms, faces, and scenarios are seen or played out in our mind's eye. Clairvoyance is similar to seeing these pictures in our mind. I will explain clairvoyance further in chapter 2.

A Séance Early One Saturday Evening

After the startling demonstration of the hand, I was convinced of the existence of God. After all, only God could manifest out of thin air. However, a whole new set of questions popped into mind. I became fascinated with the concept of death and what happens after we die. I found myself asking "what if" questions about heaven and life after death. *Is there a place where we go after we die? Is there really a heaven or hell, or a place in between? Is life infinite?* All I knew is what I had been taught in Catholic school, and that was too one-sided. *What do other people believe about God and life after death?* I wanted to understand. I wanted to know more. I wanted to investigate further. Little did I know that a supernatural adventure would come soon.

Scott and I were best friends. We played ball, and did all the other routine kid stuff together. We also experimented with the usual paranormal games that seemed to be part of growing up for most kids. We would jokingly ask questions of the Magic Eight Ball, but our grins would soon fade when answers such as *Reply hazy. Ask again later* turned up. *How could it really know?* We contacted spirits on a Ouija board, though each of us secretly believed it was the other one pushing the planchette. So it seemed only natural that one Saturday morning we decided to have a séance at seven o'clock that evening. Seven was about as close to *the witching hour* as any twelve-year-olds were going to get.

I remember that day vividly. It seemed to drag on forever. Visions of every Vincent Price movie I had ever seen flashed through my mind. Somehow, I *knew* this night was going to be special—something big was going to occur. By six-forty-five I was too anxious to wait any longer. Two hours earlier I found a white candle and stuffed it in my pocket. I thought we would need it to conduct a proper séance. I raced to Scott's house in record time. With a quick "Hello" to his parents, I hurried off with Scott to the den. I handed Scott the candle. He lit it and solemnly placed it in the center of an ashtray on a table positioned between us. We closed the windows, turned off the lights, sat facing each other, and waited. We both felt a little nervous even though we told ourselves it was all just a gag. The atmosphere was appropriately spooky. The candle created strange shadows around the room, outlining our faces with an eerie glow. The best part of this game was to see who got scared and ran first.

We sat in silence for thirty minutes. Finally, I couldn't take it anymore.

"What's next?" I asked impatiently.

Scott shrugged his shoulders. "Maybe we should ask to speak to someone."

It was the one-year anniversary of the death of Janis Joplin, so Scott suggested we call her. We chanted our call to Janis for about ten minutes. We waited. Nothing happened. We called Janis again. The candle flame remained still. There were no mysterious knocks on the table. No cold wind passed through the room. We waited some more. Our eyes constantly darted around the room, looking for any movement, any sign that Janis had arrived. But, alas, we were two twelve-year-olds getting bored.

I decided to try one last request. "Janis, if you're in the room, give us a sign with the candle," I commanded in my deepest, most melodramatic voice.

The candle flickered slightly. Suddenly, the flame leaned to the left and held there for a second. Then, it moved to the right and stayed there. Scott and I sat frozen in place. The flame began to move frantically from left to right and back again. Neither of us could breathe. Whatever moved the candle flame, it certainly was not us. We were too petrified to try anything. Suddenly the candle went out, and the room was plunged into total darkness. In a fit of bravery, we both went screaming from the room to the safety of Scott's parents.

Did we contact Janis Joplin? Who knows? I do believe we opened a door to something or someone apart from the physical world. However, I do find it ironic that what started out as a gag between two kids was a somewhat entertaining induction into what has become my career.

Other Psychic Phenomena

As I recall other events in my childhood, I had many peculiar and otherworldly experiences. I guess you could say that the séance experience was the most dramatic in a macabre sort of way. It was only one of several such experiences that I now know were definite precursors to a life intertwined with spiritualism, suspense, and mystery. The credo of my life has always been: THE UNKNOWN IS SOMETHING NOT YET FOUND. It was a part of my nature to seek out the unexplainable and find answers. Therefore, my curiosity would often take me to places where angels fear to tread. As a child, I often found a variety of games, subjects, and distractions to assist in my validation of and fascination with the occult world. A couple of my most cherished attractions were haunted houses and graveyards. Just the idea that a house supposedly contained unseen living forms roaming the hallways totally intrigued me. The natural detective in me would often take over, and I could not rest until I solved the mystery that was before me.

The Bell House was just such a mystery. A menacing structure, it was masked in chipped, antique gray paint, its worn-out shutters barely clinging to their hinges. Some were half closed over yellow-tinted windows. Bell House lived in a century that was far forgotten, when horse and buggy ruled the streets and livestock grazed lazily on the land. The house, or Manor, as it was known, was an ominous sight as it stood hidden beneath overgrown trees far from the street's pavement. To my childish eyes, it appeared as though its spires stretched straight up into the stratosphere of heaven. Bell House had been abandoned for over fifty years but had remained a daunting landmark on my way to and from school. I remember how we would run by it as fast as possible because of the stories that had evolved about it. There was the one about an old white-haired lady whose unrelenting wails were heard throughout the house.

As the story went, this lady had a son who was a sea merchant. After many idle months of not working, she insisted he go on an expedition. The son begrudgingly went and was never seen again.

It seemed there was a sudden change in the weather, and the ship on which the son sailed was destroyed in a huge storm. No one survived. His mother never accepted this explanation and thought her son ran away. From then on, she would often be seen roaming the rooms of the house looking for her boy and howling in sorrow throughout the night. Occasionally, she would leave a candle burning, hoping her son would see it and be guided home. But that was not the worst part. All of us kids knew that if we just happened to look at the house and laid our eyes on the lady's face, she would come to our bedroom at night while we were sleeping and take us back to her house to live with her forever!

My friends and I never forgot that story of Bell House, and even if it wasn't true, it certainly added a bit of excitement to our otherwise dreary walk to and from school. As I got a little older, probably around the age of ten or eleven, I pretty much discarded the harmless yarn about the old lady and her son, but I still found myself extremely fascinated with the house. I would stop in front of it and look up at the second-floor window, hoping to catch a glimmer of a burning candle or hear the soft whispers of a mumbled cry. There was definitely something in that house. I knew it. It seemed to be calling out to me, and I had to answer its call.

One day I did. My would-be mystical accomplice Scott and a couple of other brave souls from the neighborhood decided to follow my lead. Somehow, we had to find a way into the house. We decided the best way to gain access was through the back, which was practically buried under the trees. There was no fence to keep us out, so the job was easier than we first thought. After making it through the trees, our eyes fixed themselves on a decrepit, worn-out wooden house. The fortress that was once the object of so many frightful and horrendous tales appeared to be nothing more than a pile of frayed wood and outdated cement.

As luck would have it, there was a window alongside the back door. As one of the guys kept watch, the rest of us pulled a board off the window. A stream of sunshine touched a century of darkness. We carefully crawled into the house, which from the looks of it had barely made it through time. I instantly felt chills as I stood in the room. But my preconceived sense of dread and fright turned out to be feelings of joy and laughter. As I looked around, I saw what resembled a huge living room, much longer than wide. The walls were stained in yesterday's rain, and molted pink wallpaper hung torn and tattered. There were huge, gaping holes in parts of the walls that covered over wooden slats. As I walked through the room, I had a strange feeling that this was a place where dinner dances were held. I could almost see the people waltzing by. In one corner of the large room, I imagined a small band playing for the guests until the wee hours of the morning. I continued to walk straight through to an attached room on the far side. More than likely, it was a dining room large enough to accommodate a good-size crowd. I could see a banquet table full of the finest foods. Upon the table were candlelight chandeliers illuminating the evening's fare. Suddenly, I was snapped out of my reverie by the sound of my friend Kevin's scream.

"Holy cow, look at this stuff," he hollered.

When I joined Kevin and the rest of the guys in the other room, I saw what made him so excited. Strewn across the floor were various books and photographs in all shapes and sizes. Many of the books were on merchandising, trade, and seamanship. Several others were accounting ledgers containing penciled-in figures. As we simultaneously noticed the books on shipping and boating, all of our faces turned white! Together we turned toward the door, searching for our nearest means of escape. All at once we vividly remembered the early childhood tales about the merchant son and his mother. *Was it true after all?* We shuddered to think what might happen to us. *What if the place was haunted and ghosts were lurking in the hallways?* I don't know if it was a guy thing, but no one was about to show how scared he was, even though I knew we were all shaking in our shoes. We decided to stay close together and further investigate our surroundings.

I picked up a couple of pictures from the floor and looked at them. They were pictures of children. One was a baby, and the other was of two boys neatly dressed. Their resemblance clearly marked them as brothers. As I held the picture, I felt a sense that someone was standing behind me. You know that feeling—when you think someone is walking behind you. It felt exactly like that. Frightened, I immediately dropped the picture. *It was the white-haired lady coming to capture me!* Slowly, I turned my head to look behind me and saw nothing. *It must be my imagination.*

Then the oddest thing happened. I suddenly had a thought to walk to the corner of the room and pick up the photograph closest to the wall. So, I walked over, bent down, and picked up the picture. Staring back at me in the framed photograph was a glamorous-looking lady wearing a long, dark dress and holding a beautiful bouquet. She had an incredible, sweet face with deep-set eyes that seemed to look right through me. Her hair was tied in a bun held taut with a ribbon. As I held the picture close to me, I got a feeling that this was the mother of the children in the two photos. I can't describe how I knew exactly, but I just did. I looked down and saw a picture of a mustached man, his arms folded, and his eyes staring straight ahead. I picked that one up as well. As I held on to his picture, I knew that he was the lady's husband. I had this feeling that they were a family who entertained frequently. They would have been a very wealthy and influential family in the area. As I looked at other family pictures, I gathered that they had some kind of tie to politics. I could not explain my feelings to my friends, and they all thought I was crazy or had a pretty vivid imagination. But I knew there was a force of some kind pushing me toward that corner of the room. *What was it? Who was it? Why did I know this family in particular enjoyed entertaining, or that they meddled in politics? Was I being told by the ghosts who still walked the halls? Was the childhood tale of a white-haired lady and her merchant son true?*

I found out the answers to all my inquiries three years later. I'll never forget it. I was at home, and the mail had just arrived. There was a booklet from the Bayside Historical Society entitled *Bayside, Yesterday and Today*. It described how the town was first inhabited by various Indian tribes, then Dutch, and ultimately English merchants. It wasn't until I got to the part about the Bell House that my interest was aroused.

Abraham Bell, a wealthy shipping merchant, had purchased three hundred acres of land on which he built a manor for his family in 1849. His family was rather large and included two sons very close in age. It was one of the first settlements in Bayside. I read further. The Bells were part of the elite, or high society, and they often enjoyed entertaining civic officials from New York City and various politicians from Washington, DC. Fascinated, I continued reading. As I turned the next page, my eyes grew wide. Staring back from the page were photos of Mr. and Mrs. Bell—the exact same photos I had held in my hand three years earlier! They were confirmation of my feelings on that eventful visit.

My other mystifying experiences all occurred around the same age, when I was ten or eleven. During lunch break, a bunch of us would get bored and want to do something different instead of playing kick ball or jump rope with the girls. Some of the cooler guys would go into town and see how many things they could steal from the local five-and-dime without getting caught. When they returned to school in the afternoon, they would proudly display their haul—usually pens, rulers, and markers. (Great extracurricular activity for Catholic-school students!)

Anyway, since I was neither cool, nor a thief, I did what I thought was cool. A bunch of us would go to the Lawrence Cemetery. This family-owned cemetery was established in the early 1800s. It has since become an historical landmark. On one particular lunch jaunt to the cemetery I had a very interesting and intriguing experience. Two of my schoolmates and I were sitting under a tree finishing our lunch. We were thoroughly enjoying the sunny, warm spring day in the serenity of the cemetery and contemplated the idea of cutting school the rest of the day. As we debated back and forth, we suddenly heard two kids laughing not too far from us. We all looked toward the giggles, but we didn't see anything. We rationalized that it was probably some kids in a backyard nearby, and their voices had traveled. Well, after we were comfortable with that explanation, the laughter started again. We all felt very weird and a little scared. We decided to investigate the source of the laughter. As we walked toward the area, once again we heard children laughing. We still could not see anything, and reluctantly we continued to walk.

As we got closer, my buddy Peter yelled out, "Look!" We saw two little kids, a boy and a girl, who resembled each other. They looked about five and six years old. As we approached them, they ran off, and we could not find them anywhere. This is the weird part. We had visited the cemetery many times and had hardly seen anyone there, and never any young kids. We figured we better get back to school. As we turned to leave, my friend Tim screamed, "Look at this." He was staring at something. It was a tombstone with the names of two children, a sister and a brother, who died at ages four and five! *Was it an apparition?* I honestly can't say, but my friends never wanted to talk about it again.

These experiences might have foretold my future if I was able to understand them at the time. But as an otherwise normal kid, I was more interested in pursuing the likes of Little League, base-ball cards, and stoop ball.

Growing Up in Catholic School

Between stints of amusing myself with haunted houses and ceme-teries, I attended Sacred Heart Catholic School. Like many chil-dren my age, I never fully understood the concept of God. I thought God was a nice man with a beard who loved us, but if we did something wrong, he would hate us and we would burn in hell as punishment. A bit scary to a small child, don't you think? I remembered times when I sat in church and looked up at the mural above the altar. It was a beautiful, pristine picture of Jesus smiling down upon the world. I remembered thinking: *How could someone like this make you burn in hell?*

Another thing we were taught was that if we said prayers, God would hear them and answer them. Well, I don't ever remember any of my prayers being answered. I couldn't understand this con-cept at all. As a child I would constantly ask questions about God but they were seldom answered. When they were, the answers did not satisfy the original questions, and instead produced more questions. For instance, the nuns at school dressed in black habits accentuated with a white wimple. The first time I laid my eyes on the nuns in those habits, I was frightened to go to school. Those women did not look like my picture of the *wives of God*, especially dressed all in black. When I asked, "Why do you wear black?" they had no reply.

From an early age I had an awareness of heaven. Although I envisioned heaven with its pearly gates, winged angels, and so forth, I also knew it was more than that. I knew that when we went to heaven, we would see all of our friends and family who died before us. The nuns agreed that we would meet our loved ones in heaven, but they explained them away as *souls*. I never understood what a *soul* was. I knew people lived in heaven, but if people lived in heaven, *where were their souls? Was their soul a part of them?* Again, such questions baffled the nuns. Unfortunately, their standard reply was to "be quiet and don't ask so many questions." To which they added, "One day you'll find out where these souls go, and then you'll wish you hadn't asked such a question." I guess they meant that I would find out when I died.

I remember an incident in second grade that made me question God even more. I didn't have the right colored pencil for a lesson, so Sister Matilda slapped me—so hard that I went flying to the floor and lost a moment of consciousness. When I sat back in my seat, she was already on the other side of the room. It was obvious that she had little concern for my welfare. I was only seven years old at the time! I remembered thinking: *Why did she hit me? I didn't hurt anyone. I didn't do anything bad. How could someone who talks about loving one another, someone who is married to God, treat me this way?* So, from a very young age, my faith and trust in the Catholic Church soon became a delicate balance between what was preached and what was demonstrated. I remained dubious.

I stayed in Catholic school because of my strong, Irish Catholic mother. She attended mass every day and insisted it was the only way to heaven. When I asked her about other religions, she just referred to them as "those heathens." (According to the Catholic Church, the Catholic faith is the one true religion.) I didn't want to be a heathen, or burn in hell, so I remained at Sacred Heart, but I felt skeptical of those big ladies who looked a lot like penguins!

In hindsight, I can understand why the nuns were so abusive to children, and why some (not all) of the priests became alcoholics, child molesters, or had affairs. I believe it is very difficult, and somewhat inhuman, to live in a state of grace all the time. Please, we are only human! There are, of course, some who are able to live such an austere lifestyle, and all the better for them. For the majority, however, it must be impossible. No wonder there has been an enormous drop in enrollment in seminaries and novitiates. The Catholic Church has an extremely archaic belief system. In many ways, it has the mind-set of the fifteenth century. Life is ever changing and evolving. What was true for our ancestors may no longer apply to us. We continually grow and expand as beings on the earth. Instead of labeling each other according to religious beliefs, we need to see each other as one and the same. I am not saying religion is a bad thing. Quite the contrary. If most of us practiced the ideals of the religions we follow, this world would certainly be a much happier place to live. No one would be gunned down on a neighborhood street or killed in a war. No one would go hungry or be homeless. Unfortunately, I believe the leaders of religions are more interested in gaining power here on earth than preparing their flocks for salvation.

Seminary Life Was Not for Me

After eight years at Sacred Heart grade school, I attended Eymard Preparatory Seminary in Hyde Park, New York. Becoming a priest was my mother's idea, not mine. But I had always wanted to get away from my hometown, and I saw this opportunity as my chance. The seminar experience was very difficult for me. It was the first time I had been away from home, and I was homesick.

Moreover, I felt abandoned. I was fourteen years old and very depressed. Fortunately for me, I discovered that many of the other boys were going through a similar emotional adjustment. If there is one thing the Catholic Church teaches well, it is that common suffering is a great unifier. Eventually, we all got used to it.

In the seminary, I returned once again to an orderly and disciplined environment. Being sensitive, I often picked up frustrations from the priests and brothers. I felt that most of them would have preferred a secular lifestyle, but for whatever reason, they gave their lives to God. When I was a seminary student, I, too, wanted to give my life over to God, but I did not want to become a priest or brother because the lifestyle was too confining. I also felt unsure about the ideas expressed in mass as being the absolute truth. Besides, as in grammar school, I was not satisfied that my religion was entirely about God. There seemed to be too many rules and regulations and not enough demonstration of the word of God in the world. The only consistent act was the collection of monetary offerings.

In my first year at the seminary, I often thought about my questions concerning God. I always kept such thoughts to myself because I was afraid everyone would think I was nuts. Often while sitting through mass I would meditate on the idea: *Who or what is God?* When I did, the experience of the outstretched hand surrounded in light came to mind. I thought: *Was it the same hand that brought me through Catholic School? Was it the same hand that steered me to the seminary?* The more I questioned, the more unsure I felt about my religion. Why weren't these questions being answered? It wouldn't be too much longer before I finally found out.

It happened during Easter week, and specifically on Good Friday. All the artifacts on the altar had been removed, and any remaining statues, crosses, and the like had been covered with cloth. The monstrance had been placed at a side altar. (A monstrance is a very tall, gold, ornate cross that contains the consecrated hosts, or wafers, that represent the body of Christ.) All the students took turns meditating in front of the monstrance. We had no set prayers, so we relied totally on what we felt. Each student knelt or sat for thirty minutes at a time during the entire weekend.

When I sat there on Good Friday, it was probably the very first time I felt a sense of God since the experience of the hand. I sat in that small room staring at this incredible gold piece of art adorned in flowers. I kept staring at it, and after twenty minutes, I became aware that God was inside the room. Not a literal figure standing *beside me*, but a feeling of peace and tranquillity *inside me*. It was the exact feeling I had when I was eight years of age. Once again, I felt it was the proof for which I was searching, the proof that God was alive. I knew it wasn't the host in front of me. It was much greater than that. It was inside me. It spoke in my heart—not words, but feelings of an incredible love that God had for me and of which I was a part. I understood then that this feeling of God was not just to be found in a seminary or church but everywhere and in everything. *God is unlimited.* I finally had an answer and knew this was the reason why I was in the seminary. I had to take this sense of God with me. From that day on, I never questioned the existence of God. I just had to look in my own heart to see God.

After that experience, I never felt obligated to finish seminary. I knew there was nothing left to learn there. For if the teachers meant to prepare me to understand the presence of God, then they succeeded. I realized that God was a part of me and all that I do. God was love and nonjudgment, understanding and compromise, justice and honesty. I realized that we all had God inside ourselves.

Life in the seminary taught me many things, and in retrospect I am grateful for having had the experience. I discovered my own sense of self that previously had been lacking. I was forced to deal with others and recognize the good and bad in them. Ironically, the seminary also helped me to realize that Catholicism was not for me. I found something much richer and deeper to believe in—God. It was not the God who sat on a throne in heaven or the son of God who hung on a cross. It was the God of love that resided in me.

After my findings, I realized that I could not continue to worship a God encumbered by Church rules that were outdated and fickle. I could no longer believe in a mythology that centered on guilt and punishment.

I still find it a bit unbelievable that the Catholic Church teaches this stuff. Please don't get me wrong. Everyone is entitled to believe the way he or she sees fit. I am just referring to my own background.

Communication with the Other Side

I left the seminary after my first year and spent the next three years in a New York City public high school. I moved out of the house once again when I entered San Francisco State College to major in broadcasting. I dreamed of a career as a screenwriter. As luck would have it, while coordinating a conference with the creative staff of *Hill Street Blues*, I became friendly with one of the show's producers. When I told him I would be graduating soon, he offered what I thought was my first big break. I'll never forget those magic words: "Call me when you get to L.A. We can probably put you on the show as a production assistant." *A production assistant!* Suddenly, my life was on a roll.

After graduation, I wasted little time when I returned to New York. I bought a car, packed my gear, and headed west. I rolled into Los Angeles on July 7, 1982. At last I was in the major leagues. I made it to Hollywood! I vowed that I would not leave Tinsel Town until I realized my dream and became a writer. I called my friend, the producer, to let him know I was ready to begin my new life. He was not available.

I survived as a temp until I worked my way full-time into the basement of the William Morris Agency. I had the glamorous responsibility of pulling staples out of files that were being prepared for microfiche. I spent most of my time daydreaming about being a famous screenwriter and living the glamorous life. Even though my present situation was not my dream job, I had the strangest sensation in the pit of my stomach that it was important for me to stay where I was. Very soon, I knew why.

One day, my supervisor, Carol Shoemaker, and I were discussing metaphysics. She had an appointment to see a medium named Brian Hurst. "Do you want to come with me?" she asked. I had no idea what a medium was, but I jumped at the chance to leave the mail room and discover something new.

We arrived in Manhattan Beach a few minutes before our seven o'clock appointment time. *Maybe seven was the witching hour after all.* I felt a little nervous about the whole thing. My mind kept skipping back to the séance with Scott and Janis. I started to wonder if contacting the dead was such a good idea.

I was not calmed by the smiling Englishman with the large green eyes who met us at the door. When he introduced himself, I thought he seemed a little too pleasant for his line of work. As we walked into his home, my mind raced double time, conjuring up images of demons that this sorcerer might unleash. Nonetheless, Carol and I settled into a comfortable spot on the bright orange couch. Were we ready for the ride? I wasn't so sure.

Brian spent the next half hour describing what we were going to experience. He explained that he was *clairaudient*—he was literally able to *hear* spirit voices in his ear. He said, "The spirit people are on a very fast vibration. They speak very quickly. Sometimes it sounds like Morse code. I get pieces of information like blips and bleeps." Upon ending this explanation, he told Carol that her father was standing in the corner of the room. "He looks like he injured his finger."

Carol responded that her father had cut his finger right before he died. I was flabbergasted. *How did he know this?* I sat at the edge of my seat and waited to hear more.

Brian continued to talk about Carol's father. There were no moving candles or tapping tables, however.

Twenty minutes later, Brian turned to me. He said that there was another James in spirit who gave me his love and had an interest in my life. I had no idea to whom he was referring. Later, I learned that I did have an uncle James who had died some years back.

Near the end of the session, Brian said, "You know, James, you are very mediumistic. The spirit people are telling me that one day you will give readings like this to other people. The spirits are planning to use you."

I wasn't sure how to respond to this pronouncement. After all, my goals were in a completely different direction. I wasn't ready for my life to take a 180-degree turn. With some nervousness, I replied, "I have enough trouble understanding the living. Why would I want to start talking to the dead?"

Brian simply smiled and calmly assured me, "One day you will."

The Exploration of My Own Psychic Powers

For months after our session, Brian's prediction haunted me. At that time, he continued to explain that not everyone was able to raise their vibration to a level that would allow for direct communication with those in spirit. "Fortunately for you, James, you would be able to make such an adjustment."

I was fascinated by Brian's contact with the spirit world and curious about his assessment of my ability to do the same thing. The curiosity from my childhood charged to the forefront. *Why me? What had I done to qualify for this?* In my heart, I knew that this was to be my future life, and all my experiences were preparing me for this turn of events. However, my head could not reconcile such an outlandish prospect. After all, it was not exactly the life I had planned. *What about my writing career? Isn't that the reason I am in Los Angeles? Could there be another plan for me?* I decided to evaluate my psychic abilities and see for myself.

I bought every book I could find having to do with psychic or mediumistic development. Many of the books described different techniques for enhancing the natural psychic ability we all have.

Some of the techniques described were as follows: I had to hold an object, close my eyes, and see what *feelings* came up about the object. These *feelings* could be in the form of pictures, sounds, names, or emotions. Another technique was to hold a picture of one person or several people and write on a piece of paper any thoughts about the people in the picture, such as their ages, their likes and dislikes, whether they were happy, sad, tense, worried about something, and the like. One of the exercises involved an entire group of people. One person had to sit in a chair facing away from the group. Another person would stand about two feet behind the person in the chair. Then the person in the chair was to describe everything he or she felt about the person standing. Was it a male or female energy? What were the person's outstanding features? Describe the person's clothes. Did the person wear glasses?

All of these exercises were designed to help me use my feelings instead of my head to sense the world around me. I was soon incorporating several of the exercises into my everyday life. For instance, on the way to the office, I would try to guess which elevator would arrive first. Or I would try to intuitively see the colors of my coworkers' clothes for that day. The more often I used my intuition, the more often my guesses were correct.

On several occasions, I found these exercises quite useful and fun at the same time. I remember arranging a meeting in the conference room where I worked and trying to guess how many people would attend. My first impression was the number twenty-four. So without asking anyone, I set up twenty-four chairs and twenty-four glasses of water. By now, many of my coworkers knew about my psychic games, so they were not at all surprised to see the room prearranged. After the room was in order, the group started to promenade through the door. One by one they sat down until the total reached twenty-two. I thought, *How could I be off by two?* My coworker, Jodie, looked at me and winked, as if to say *Better luck next time.* Needless to say, I bowed my head in disappointment. Five minutes into the meeting, the supervisor announced the hiring of a new employee. The door opened and there stood Mr. Ryan and his secretary Carmen. They sat in the remaining two chairs. I looked over at Jodie and winked back: *I told you so.*

As I became more confident with the intuition I had developed, I began to read people. This was my way of tuning into them on an emotional level. I guess you could call it a gut reaction. It worked the same way as the exercise with the pictures. I attempted to feel what was going on inside a person. Was she a good person? Was she hiding something? Was he happy or sad? What were her desires in life? What motivated him? I registered my feelings and then looked at the physical person to see if what I picked up intuitively matched him or her physically. At first, it took some time to figure out what questions to ask myself. But after a while, it seemed to take just seconds to read someone.

Once again, I found that the more often I followed my first instinct, the more often I was right. I had to learn not to be afraid to ask myself: *Was the feeling I received colored by my own bias or judgment? Was it my very first feeling, or had I thought about it too much?* It quickly became clear to me that learning to trust my hunches and to follow my initial instinct was valuable regardless of my reasons for doing it or where the road of life led me.

Within a year of beginning my intuitive exercise program, my sensitivity had increased dramatically. People at work started to call me at home to ask questions about the future. Most of the questions concerned relationships, and those vibrations were the easiest to read. At least I could immediately feel if there was something wrong. I began to get mental images of the faces of the people under discussion. I could describe the color of their hair and eyes, their jawline, sometimes right down to a birthmark. Almost every time I described the physical characteristics of the significant other over the phone, I was inevitably correct. I could also tell the type of emotional involvement the two shared.

For instance, I once read for a woman named Paula over the phone. When she asked me about her boyfriend, Michael, I immediately tuned into her on an emotional vibration and felt her as being alone. (It is much easier to do this on the phone because the physical appearance doesn't get in the way of feelings.) I told her that I felt she was emotionally alone and that she desperately desired to have a balanced and normal relationship with Michael, but he was not emotionally available to her. She answered, "Yes." I further said that he was not only emotionally distant but often not physically around. (When one is in a relationship with another person, each partner's energy stays with the other. If a couple does not spend a lot of physical time together, the energy around the other person dissipates significantly.)

On another occasion, a young woman called Cindy asked me what I thought about her fiancé. I felt Cindy's energy over the phone and asked for the name of her fiancé. I tuned into his name alongside of her energy and felt a total imbalance. I told her that I didn't think he was a good choice. I suggested she put the marriage off for a little while. She said, "You are totally wrong," and that was the end of that. Two years later, a friend happened to remind me of my phone conversation with Cindy. She told me that Cindy did indeed marry the young man three months later. The marriage lasted five months, and the couple just recently filed for divorce.

I don't want you to get the impression that I'm never wrong. Of course I am. I just want to explain that for me the easiest way to read someone is through the emotions. The emotions are the rawest of energies, and whether they realize it or not, most people wear their hearts on their sleeves.

As time went by, the more I used my intuitive feelings, the stronger they became, and the more I learned to trust them. Soon, friends, then friends of friends, called to ask questions about their lives. It never occurred to me to ask for money from any of them because I was still learning. Besides, I was getting a high just having my impressions verified. It was during this period of self-imposed intuitive development that Brian's prediction of spirit communication revealed itself. I was speaking to a young lady on the telephone about her problem. Suddenly, I had an overwhelming desire to ask her if she knew a Helen.

"Yes," she replied. "Helen is my grandmother. She died a while ago."

I continued, "She is giving me a thought of Idaho."

The girl said, "Yes, that's where she lived!"

"Your grandmother is telling me that she used to do needle-point and had made some cushions for her couch. She says she was insistent that her footstool stay in the right place all the time. She also says that she loves to look at the beautiful rose pattern on the footstool. Helen wants you to know that she has made a similar one in heaven."

There was a long silence on the other end of the phone. The girl was shocked, but she verified that everything I relayed to her was true. I hung up the phone and immediately took two aspirin. I could not believe it was actually happening. Brian's prediction had come true—I had actually talked to spirits. Even with all my studying and all of the verification, I was not prepared for that moment. A whole new world of incredible feeling and understanding had opened to me. The possibilities were thrilling; the responsibilities, enormous.

I learned that when I raised my vibration to reach into the other side, the connection infused me with incredible sensations of freedom—love and joy. It was that same sense of God that filled me as a young boy. Keeping up the vibration exhausted me, but the rewards were well worth it. The difficulty came when the session was over and I had to relate once again to a three-dimensional, physical world. I would have to practice a new balancing act to stay sane.

The requests for readings began to pour in. I never solicited clients—they all came by word of mouth. Soon, the requests were so overwhelming that I knew I had to make a choice. *Should I stay with my new job in the contracts department at Paramount Studios, or should I practice the gift I had been given on a full-time basis?* Actually, it was never a choice. So many of my experiences had led me to that moment. I simply had to have the courage and self-confidence to take the next step. And, so I did.

In the past decade I have had the great fortune to speak to

thousands of people through individual readings, group meetings, international symposiums, and more recently on radio and television. The experiences, some of which you will read about in this book, have been extremely gratifying, intensely emotional, and overwhelmingly positive. I have learned to let go of my ego desires, and allow my life to flow in whatever direction it takes me. It has certainly been an exciting adventure. And I can't wait to see what's next.

What I Believe

Since the experience of the hand when I was eight, and the years in Catholic schools, I have been on a spiritual quest. On my journey, I have often been asked if I believe in the existence of God, or heaven and hell. Based on my spiritual communication work and the hundreds of books I have read, I have come to the following conclusions.

First of all, I do believe in God. In fact, I believe we are all God. What does that mean? Well, I believe that we are all made in the likeness of God. I am speaking not of our human qualities but of our spiritual qualities. Although we appear differently on the outside, we are the same inside. When we become aware of the spiritual person, we begin to see the God Light within that person, and with this wisdom we begin to realize that we are all one and the same. We are all made of the *God spark*. Even the lowest creature crawling on the ground is made from the same *God spark*. Even those who appear evil and bad are made of this same *God spark*. The beings who are evil are perhaps the furthest from that which is God. God is perfection in everything. God is creativity in all things. Each one of us is perfect if we would only seek our divinity. However, the majority of us get caught up in the "ego" self, or the human part of ourselves, so that we rarely come close to the truth of who we are.

Where does God reside? My answer is: within you. Within the very core of you. God is your essence. God is life itself. I don't believe that God is a figure in space looking down on us. And while there have been many who have represented the great Light of God in human form, the same *God spark* that was in them is in each one of us. God is my light, your light, and everyone else has this same light, too. The difference may be in the degree—some lights are brighter than others, and some lights are very dim.

Secondly, I believe in heaven. I personally believe that heaven is the other side of our physical world and is very much like our physical world with similar sights and sounds, although more vivid and more colorful. Heaven is a place where we can stroll in a garden, or ride a bicycle, or row a boat. As a matter of fact, we can do anything in heaven that we want as long as we have earned it. However, many of us have been filled with the idea of a "Christian" heaven. I have often asked myself: *Where do the Muslims or the Jews go when they die?* Certainly not to a Christian heaven! Suffice to say, each religion has a heaven and hell based on their particular beliefs.

I believe there are many levels to heaven, and we go to that level we have created by our thoughts, words, and deeds while on earth. Those of us who have grown to the same spiritual level will reside with one another in the same heaven. Beings who are more spiritually aware reside on a higher level, and less evolved souls are on a lower level. We can never go to a higher level until we earn it. However, those beings on a higher level can go to a lower sphere, and in many cases, they do just that in order to aid and assist those souls who are not as aware. So where do bad or evil people go? They go to the heaven, or the hell, that they have created based upon their words, thoughts, and deeds while on earth. They, too, exist with other beings who are on their level of spiritual evolvement.

In this book, I hope to clarify these beliefs so that your questions about God and the spirit world may be answered as mine were.

CHAPTER 2

The Gift

What is energy? Energy is everything. To define it in very simple terms, energy is made of molecules rotating or vibrating at various rates of speed. In our physical world, molecules rotate at a very slow rate of speed. Also, everything in this physical world vibrates at a constant speed. That is why things on earth appear to be solid. The slower the speed, the more dense or solid the thing, for example, the chair in which you are sitting, this book you are reading, the house in which you live, and, of course, your physical body. Beyond our three-dimensional world, the molecules vibrate at a much faster or higher rate of speed. Therefore, in such a subtle environment, or ethereal dimension, as the spirit world, things are freer and less dense.

Within our physical body is another body usually called the *astral, etheric,* or *spirit* body. This body is an exact replica of our physical body in that it contains eyes, hair, hands, legs, and so on. The big difference between our physical and etheric bodies is that the etheric body's molecules vibrate at a much faster and higher rate than its physical counterpart. Typically, we can't see the astral body, although some people are able to see it psychically. During the transition called death, this etheric body is released or freed from the physical body. The etheric body has no disease or fatigue that once was a part of the physical body, and it has the ability to move from one point to another through thought.

A Medium May Have a Variety of Abilities

Those who are able to tune into the faster vibration of the spirit body after death, either in a physical or a mental way, are called *sensitives* or *mediums*. As the term suggests, a medium is an individual who is a middleman or mediator, a person who goes between the spiritual and physical worlds. A medium is able to use energy to reach through the thin veil separating the physical life from the spiritual life. A way of looking at the concept of mediumship is as follows: Human beings are made of the superconscious, the subconscious, and the conscious minds. In mediumship all thoughts, feelings, and sights are transmitted through a medium's superconscious, or spirit mind. We all are constantly picking up spirit impressions in this way, but it is the medium who is able to interpret them. The message then moves into the conscious mind and is revealed.

The term "psychic" is often used as a catchall phrase for anyone who works in the paranormal. Everyone is psychic to some degree or another, but not everyone is a medium. A medium is *not* a fortune teller. In other words, mediums are psychic, but not all psychics are mediums. Psychism and mediumship use the same mechanics of the mind, but mediumship differs from "being psychic," or psychism. Like mediumship, psychism is telepathic. Telepathy is another word for mind-to-mind communication. For example, you are with a friend, and you say exactly what he is thinking. Your friend responds by saying, "You must be psychic." A person who is psychic is able to read an inanimate object or a person by tuning into the energy that emanates from the object or person. It is in this aura of the object or person that a psychic interprets revelations of the past and the future of the item or person. A psychic may also receive the energy of the object or person by feeling or seeing. Because there is no time in the energy world, few psychics can give an accurate time frame about the information received.

On the other hand, a medium, or sensitive, is a person who is able to feel and/or hear thoughts, voices, or mental impressions from the spirit world. Spirits also use telepathy. A medium is able to become completely receptive to the higher frequencies or energies on which spirit people vibrate. Hence, the mind of a spirit melds or impresses itself on the superconscious mind of a medium. From there, the message goes into the conscious mind, and a medium reveals what a spirit is thinking or feeling. Mediumship is much more involved than basic psychism because a medium is opening him/herself to a discarnate energy. In psychism, the information does not come from a discarnate spirit who resides on a higher frequency level. A discarnate uses much of a medium's life energy to send its message. A medium works directly with a spirit, and the two have to be willing to take part in the communication process; otherwise there is no communication.

The concept of mediumship is more easily apparent in dreams. Many times we dream of relatives or friends who have passed over. The dream feels so real that we swear we were indeed with them. We feel strongly about it. This is because while in our dream state we were actually with our loved ones on a spiritual plane. When we sleep, our etheric or astral body travels in nonearthly realms where we encounter our loved ones and are able to communicate with them.

Mediumship itself can be broken down into two distinct categories. The first and most common type is mental mediumship. As the word *mental* denotes, this form of mediumship utilizes the mind—the intuitive or cosmic mind, not the rational or logical part. This type of mental mediumship falls into several distinct types: clairvoyance, clairaudience, clairsentience, and inspirational thought.

Clairvoyance

Derived from the French language, *clairvoyance* means "clear vision." A clairvoyant applies her innate sense of inner sight to see objects, colors, symbols, people, spirits, or scenes. These pictures are not visible to the naked eye and usually flash into the medium's mind as if she were physically seeing. In most cases the sights should be recognizable to the person for whom she is reading, whom I refer to as the *sitter*.

Clairaudience

This term means "clear hearing." A clairaudient hears with the psychic ear or sensitized ear. He is able to hear sounds, names, voices, and music that vibrate on a higher frequency. Much like dogs that hear at a higher frequency range than humans, mediums, too, hear beyond our normal hearing range. A clairaudient provides the sitter exactly what he hears from that higher rate of vibration. Although he hears the actual spirit voices or whispers with the same inflection the person would have used on the earth, he tells the sitter in his own voice what he is hearing.

Clairsentience

This is a form of mental mediumship that means "clear feeling." A medium with clairsentience is able to sense when spirits are in the room. A true clairsentient will usually feel the *spirit personality* coming through his entire being. He is able to give messages to the sitter by way of strong, empathetic feelings and emotions from the spirit. In clairsentience, not only is the mind of a medium used but a medium's emotional body as well.

Inspirational Thought

This is also known as inspirational speaking, inspirational writing, or inspirational art. In inspirational thought, a medium receives thoughts, impressions, knowledge—all without forethought. It differs from clairsentience because the emotional state is *not* as evident in inspirational thought as it is with a *spirit personality* coming through to speak. Inspirational thought is very objective.

It has neither the intense emotions nor the spirit personality attached to the message. These are associated with clairsentience. Although inspirational thought comes from spirit, the personality of a spirit is not impressed on the receiver.

In many cases, a band or group of souls can impress an earthly recipient with inspirational thought. This group of souls melds their thoughts together and impresses the person to write a certain piece of music or paint a particular picture. Again, this is not done on an emotional level; rather, it is purely through inspiration. Many great artists such as Michelangelo, Monet, and Renoir, and musicians like Bach, Mozart, and Schubert were mediums. Great scientists and doctors of the past were also mediums utilizing inspirational thought. All around us today, we have wonderful artists, musicians, writers, actors, and speakers who use the mental mediumistic art of inspirational thought.

The second type of mediumship is physical mediumship, and it differs from mental mediumship. In physical mediumship, the actual physical body is used; in mental mediumship, only the mind of the medium is utilized. Channeling is a well-known form of physical mediumship.

There is a substance that emanates from our bodies known as ectoplasm. *Ectoplasm* is from the Greek: *ektos,* meaning "outside" or "external," and *plasma*, meaning "something molded or formed." Ectoplasm was discovered by Dr. Charles Richet, a French professor of physiology, after he viewed a misty substance emanating from the bodies of several mediums. Ectoplasm is invisible, yet it varies in its states of denseness. It can appear as a gas, a liquid, or more commonly, as sort of a cheesecloth substance. It is colorless, odorless, and its weight is said to be about 8.6 grams per liter, or less than one ounce in liquid measurement. Ectoplasm is found in most people, but it is especially developed in mediums. It can be seen mainly in a dark setting, since the substance is extremely sensitive to light. Ectoplasm can emerge out of a medium's ears, mouth, nose, or solar plexus area. This stringy, gauzelike material can be utilized in a variety of ways, such as the following.

Voice Box

In this particular mediumship, ectoplasm is molded to form an artificial voice box and through it emanates the voice of a spirit. The sound is similar to, or exactly like, the voice of a person while he or she was alive on the earth. I attended four séances where this phenomenon was present. I was fortunate to sit with the famous English physical medium Leslie Flynt. In his day, Leslie had many celebrities in his séance room. Among the most frequent was Mae West, who would herself hold séances on a regular basis. At my third sitting with Leslie, my mother came through, and she sounded identical to the way she did on earth. She called me by my nickname, which no one else knew except the two of us. The experience was, to say the least, inspiring and unforgettable. Unfortunately, this type of mediumship is rare, and I know only one other medium in the world still alive who can create such a phenomenon.

Materialization

This is the rarest form of physical mediumship, and the most amazing. Those in spirit can form anything from partial limbs, faces, heads, and torsos, to complete bodies that are exact replicas of the deceased as they appeared on earth. The denseness of the materialization depends strongly on the medium's own developed state. There were many famous materialization mediums earlier in this century. Among them were Jack Webber, Ethel Post-Parrish, and Helen Duncan.

Apports

An *apport* is a phenomenon in which various objects such as jewelry, flowers, coins, and the like materialize in a séance room. One of the beliefs behind an apport is that an object dematerializes in one place and materializes in another. Another belief is that an object is formed directly by the spirit world.

Spiritual Healing

Another form of physical mediumship is spiritual healing. A medium's body is imbued with healing energy from the spirit world. After much practice, a medium can cure many incurable diseases and maladies. This is different from *magnetic healing* whereby the actual vital forces of a medium are used for healing work.

Spirit Photography

This type of mediumship is more common. Phantomlike figures or exact replications of deceased people appear on photographs. One may also see whitish spots, "lights," or "flashes" on the photographs.

I am a mental medium, utilizing the gifts of clairsentience and clairvoyance. I usually tell the sitter that I am merely a telephone to the spirit world. Just as we all receive thoughts on a daily basis, I am aware of and sensitive to thought frequencies that the spirit people create and send to my consciousness. In order to attune to the thoughts and feelings of a spirit, I have to raise my vibrations higher and, in turn, a spirit has to lower its vibrations somewhat. Sometimes, this can be very difficult. Usually I don't hear in complete sentences as I can in normal conversation with human beings. When a spirit says, "Hello, how are you today," I may hear "lo, are yo day."

When I sit with a client, it is important that the energy of the room be harmonious to both the sitter and myself. I prefer to perform my sittings in my home, where the conditions are balanced, peaceful, quiet, and pleasant. When a sitter enters the room, I can tell immediately if he or she is nervous, angry, apprehensive, scared, meditative, open, or closed. In other words, I can feel the energy surrounding the sitter. If need be, I have the person relax by doing a brief meditation. After the meditation, and when the person feels more at ease, I explain how I work and what to expect. Clients are allowed to tape-record their sessions with me.

Spirit Communication

When I feel the subtle energies around me shift, I relax and open my mind to the thoughts of those attempting to communicate. I repeat to the sitter exactly what I receive without thinking or trying to interpret the words. Even though the thought may not make sense to me, more than likely it will be understood by the sitter. Even though I try not to analyze what I am hearing, sometimes I do. However, I have to constantly remind myself that what may sound insignificant to me may be of utmost importance to the sitter.

Also, as a clairsentient, I can feel the death condition associated with the individual making contact. When the spirit returns to the earth atmosphere, it picks up the memory associated with its last time on the physical plane. For almost all, it is the death condition that is the most vivid. As an example, if a person passed over from a heart attack, I may experience a spiritual presence through a gripping pain across my chest. If someone died of cancer or AIDS, I may feel a sense of wasting away in my body. If a death occurred suddenly, like a murder, there may be a jolt through my body. If a death was by suicide, my feeling will be based on the method of self-destruction. In other words, if someone took pills, I may feel a heaviness in my stomach and a sudden sense of drowsiness. If a person shot himself, I may feel a sharp pain in the area where the bullet entered. My primary impressions manifest on an emotional level. Therefore, if a spirit is upset and crying, I may suddenly feel depressed and begin to cry. If a spirit laughs and jokes, I will also begin to laugh.

The personality of a spirit almost always accompanies the emotional thought being sent. For instance, if a spirit had an authoritative personality on earth, the tone of my voice may become commanding. If a personality had a sharp tongue, I may speak with this trait. If the individual was very unemotional and closed off to feelings and not very demonstrative, it may take much more effort on my part as the medium to describe something emotionally.

Usually, spirits will transmit messages that the sitter easily understands. At the beginning of communication, a spirit will give his or her name, or where he or she lived, or some insignificant fact that provides evidential proof to the sitter that the loved one is present. Many times, spirits will furnish trivial information known only to the sitter. By way of an example, a sitter's grandmother might say that she likes the flowered blanket covering his couch. Or she might talk about the boxes of books that the sitter recently unpacked and placed upon the second shelf of his bookcase.

Many people ask me why spirits come through with such trivial data when there is a whole new realm of existence of which they can speak. The answer is very simple: It is the simple revelation that verifies a spirit exists and is indeed communicating with the sitter.

Also, if a spirit was interested in a particular hobby or activity while on earth, it will more than likely reveal this interest during the reading. For instance, I had a client whose deceased husband told her that she must make sure to fill the yellow bird feeder that hung on their backyard tree. She said, "My God, that's him. He would go out every morning and put seeds in that feeder. I can't believe it. He's right. I forgot to put the seeds in this week; it's been so crazy." To anyone else, this thought might seem quite trivial, but to the sitter it was corroboration that she was indeed speaking to her husband. Names are one thing, but minor details only help to demonstrate that the communication between a spirit and the sitter is authentic. It provides the necessary proof that the spirit is who he says he is.

One must realize that when someone passes to the other side of life, it does not mean that he or she has learned all the secrets of the universe. At death, only the physical body is shed, much like discarding an old overcoat. In fact, the personality remains the same, complete with likes, dislikes, prejudices, talents, and attitudes. In time, a spirit might progress to a higher spiritual level and perhaps enlighten itself, but this, too, is strictly up to the individual. Also, we must understand that a spirit's knowledge of things in general is slightly above our physical comprehension.

Spirits Cannot Interfere with Karmic Progression

Many clients come to me seeking information from spirits regarding wealth, love, or career. Usually, I tell them that they might be disappointed. The spirit people may or may not be able to provide such information. It all depends on whether the spirit knows the answer, and also whether the spirit is allowed to reveal it. When a soul comes on this earth to learn certain lessons or to spiritually progress, the last thing he or she needs is for a spirit being to give the answers to a situation that may be a test. We must be aware that there are spiritual laws, and a spirit being cannot interfere or try to influence the spiritual or karmic progression of another. So, certain types of information may be veiled or hidden from the sitter. The spirit people love us too much to hinder our growth.

By spiritual lessons, let me explain further through the following:

A woman named Marcie came to see me, and her first question was whether or not she was going to have a baby. Her grandfather came through, and he said to her,

"You will first change residence and move to a place high above the water, and then have a baby boy. Not before!"

She replied, "But I'm in my forties. What am I going to do?"

He said, "It will occur in God's time, not yours."

Marcie was given further information about her move and her family. She was told it would all happen when the time was right. A year and a half later, Marcie paid me another visit. She informed me that she had recently moved to a house above the Pacific Ocean and was three months pregnant.

Another case involved a girl named Nancy, who had recently filed for divorce. Nancy's mother came through and told her that she would leave her current husband but would marry again—this time to someone who would be much more compatible.

Nancy asked, "Where will I meet this man and what does he look like?"

Her mother replied, "It is not right for me to tell you that, but know that it is true."

The mother wasn't able to tell her daughter the answers to these vital questions because the girl had to go through the process of living and make some challenging decisions for herself. Perhaps these decisions would help her grow in her own personal strength and power.

Successful communication takes place if there is a strong desire by both the sitter and the spirit. We can all communicate to our dearly departed. All we need is to have an open mind and a mutual understanding of love and energy. When we do, wondrous discoveries are within reach.

In chapters 10 and 11, I explain how we can prepare ourselves to be receptive to mediumship and give various exercises and methods to attune ourselves to the higher worlds.

CHAPTER 3

Spiritual Helpers

Humankind has always believed in the existence of higher beings or angels. Although mythological in concept, the idea of someone to watch over us is a widely accepted belief. According to religious texts, an angel is a spiritually evolved entity who exists in a heavenly plane and guards us against impending danger or disaster. Most of us were first introduced to the idea of angels as small children, when we were told that we have our very own guardian angel.

The idea of a guardian angel is one of the few truisms that organized religion has not destroyed. For indeed, we do have guardian angels or guides who intervene for us and assist in our earthly missions, but not in the ways they are so often depicted. In other words, our guides or angels do *not* have wings, nor do they sit on clouds and play harps. These images originated in mythology and were embellished in paintings by artists. Actually, wings are the beautiful bands of color that encircle an angel. You might say, it is the angel's *aura* or energy field, something that surrounds every living being, from plants, animals, and trees to ourselves and our own precious earth.

Spirit Guides Are Unique for Each Person

There are many types of guides, and to me, guardian angels and guides are one and the same. Before we were born, we mapped out a blueprint for our life's journey. When we veer off our life's path, usually a guide will help us to get back on track. Depending on our individual spiritual evolution and earthly work ahead, we will draw to us various helpers from three distinct categories.

The first group of guides are *personal guides*. These are persons we have known in previous incarnations or in between lifetimes with whom we share an affinity. These guides assist us from spiritual realms by impressing our minds with ways to involve ourselves in certain situations. These impressions are signs from our spirit guides. Most of the time, these subtle indicators go unnoticed. But if we take the time to stop and listen and evaluate our day, we may begin to see and/or hear spirit's messages.

For most people, it is difficult to feel guidance from spirit because they want and/or expect blatant directives, as if Gabriel were to blow his horn. I'm sorry, but it doesn't quite work that way. Messages and/or guidance are subtle and gentle contact.

The following is an example of how spirit communication generally works. It's Thursday, and you have a meeting with a potential partner regarding a business proposition. On the way, you either lose the address or you get lost trying to find the place. This seems quite odd to you because you are very familiar with this part of town. After a half hour of driving around, you locate the building, but now you can't find a parking place. You finally find one several blocks away. When you arrive at the building, the front entrance is locked, so you search for another way inside. A security guard opens the door, and you take the elevator to the designated floor. When you get off, the office is locked, and a note taped to the door gives direction to another office on another floor. You finally find the office and meet your prospective business partner. You listen to the deal and throughout the conversation, you have a gnawing feeling in the pit of your stomach. You feel something, but you're not sure what it is. Nevertheless, you agree to go into business. Several months later, after investing all your life's savings into this business, your new partner skips town with all your money and any trace of what turned out to be a phony business scam.

I realize that I have taken this scenario to the nth degree, but I wanted to point out just how spirit guidance works. There is a pattern to this story—too many incorrect turns, wrong directions, and closed doors. If you had taken the time to observe the subtle clues, you would have understood that *someone was trying to tell you something!* Your spirit guides were trying to warn you!

Unfortunately, too many of us go through life in a fog and usually need to be hit over the head with a baseball bat to become aware of what is going on around us.

On the positive side, spirit communication might go something like this: For some time, you have been looking for a job, but with no luck. A friend from whom you haven't heard in quite a while calls you and asks you to lunch. You check your calendar and note that the only day you have available is the day she suggests. When you meet her, it's as if you never lost touch. Everything feels perfect. You tell her your predicament, and she says she'll keep an eye out for you. A day later, your friend calls and tells you that a position in a nearby department just became available. You immediately call for an interview using your friend as a referral. An appointment is easily made for the next day. You get to the interview with plenty of time to spare. During your interview, the head of the department, who is usually out of town, is available to interview you right there on the spot. She meets you, likes you, and you get the job.

Do you see the difference? Everything in the second example happened serendipitously. I don't think there is anything like coincidence or luck. Our spirit guides draw to us what we have earned. The person looking for a job took action with the signs from spirit. She had the free will not to meet her friend, but she chose to do so. Her guides were communicating, and she had the sense to follow. After that, everything seemed to fall into place.

Often, I receive similar helpful messages when I do readings for people. I remember telling a sitter that he had recently bought a house, to which he replied, "Yes." I told him that everything about the house seemed perfect, and if he could recall the way he got the house, it was a bit bizarre. I said, "Either someone fell out of escrow, or the lender bent over backwards to assist you." His reply was again, "Yes. That was exactly what happened." I told him that his deceased wife helped him to get the house by giving him signs along the way. He said, "Everything seemed so easy." He really just followed through on the signs, although he may not have been consciously aware of them.

One of the very first psychics I met in Los Angeles told me something quite profound. I remember it to this day and will share it with you. *If everything is going right and there seems to be no glitches, you are open to spirit and following your guidance. If, on the other hand, nothing seems to be working out, you are not listening to the guides and will end up on the wrong path.* Very true.

A personal guide might also be someone you have known in this lifetime. For instance, it might be a mother or father, a grandparent, an aunt or uncle, or a friend who has passed into the spirit world. When someone passes over, he or she does not stop thinking of you. The love bond created on earth continues in the spirit world.

Once in heaven, a spirit might review her life and see how she should have done more to help you while she was alive. Now that she has the opportunity, she can take full advantage of it and will provide support in any way she can. This might be in the form of helping with daily events, or family concerns, or supporting you through personal upsets or changes.

Personal guides may make vigorous attempts to guide us through our daily lives and impress us with the best way to remedy certain situations. However, at the same time it is important to note that these loved ones cannot and do not interfere with those lessons or challenges that we have created on earth from which to learn and grow. Our learning process is never an easy one, and in order for us to get the most benefit from a particular situation or life lesson, many times these guides just stand by and watch us make our decisions. Even though at times it seems things are unbearable, it is at those times that we learn the most.

Many people ask if our guides are with us all the time or whether we have to reach out to them and ask them to come through. My answer is: We are never alone. Our guides are with us always. Their spiritual task is to watch over us and assist us. Our guides may change from time to time depending on the task in which we are involved. But we never need to call them, for they know our needs and are always ready to lend us a hand.

The second category is made up of *mastery* or *specialized* helpers. These are spirits who are drawn to us based on certain activities or work in which we are engaged. Mastery guides possess a certain expertise in a field that we are endeavoring to undertake. Usually, these beings are experts in their particular fields of knowledge. For instance, if you decide to write a mystery story, your thoughts will draw to you an author who has worked or has specialized in that particular type of writing. This guide may impress your mind with certain ways to develop your writing skills and best carry out your ideas. The same is true for musicians, artists, mathematicians, scientists, teachers, social workers, and others. Particular guides are drawn to us or will come if we ask for assistance. The more open you are to your impressions and feelings, the more successful the transmission and the end result. This is true for everyone. It is simply a matter of our being receptive. All work, especially that of the great masters, is inspired by the spirit world.

Why do these guides want to help us? The answer is simple: It is the way. When we pass into the world of spirit we become keenly aware that we are all equally one. We want to help humankind to grow, to learn, to share ideas, to better itself. By impressing their thoughts upon humans and aiding them, spiritual guides help humankind to tune into the spiritual force in all things. Again, depending on how open we are, spirit inspirations may be exceptional and awe-inspiring, or they might be patiently waiting for the day when they are noticed.

The third category of helpers contains our *spirit* or *master teachers*. These individuals may be quite spiritually evolved, or may never have lived in the physical world, or may have been involved in some aspect of spiritual work during many lifetimes upon this earth. Like our other guides, they, too, gravitate to us based upon our level of spiritual evolution and understanding. Spirit teachers have a strong desire to help us in our spiritual progression. They often try to impress upon us our spiritual gifts and potentialities. This guidance is immeasurable to anyone who is on the path to spiritual enlightenment.

Most of us will have one or two of the same master teachers throughout our soul's evolution lifetime after lifetime. These beings are tuned into our spiritual selves and will help us to grow spiritually throughout our time on the physical plane, as well as assist us in between lives. In addition, we will have individual master guides during a particular lifetime. Once again, based on our soul's evolution, a guide is drawn to us to help with important lessons or aspects of our personalities that need to be perfected. For example, we might have a guide to assist us in learning unconditional love. Or a master guide may help us in lessons about selfishness. The saying "When the student is ready, the teacher will appear" is quite true.

Becoming Aware of My Guides

I have become aware of my own guides and teachers through several different means. Once, a gifted clairvoyant by the name of Irene Martin-Giles in England informed me that there was a nun from the order of Sisters of Mercy who works with me to learn compassion. Her name is Sister Theresa. The clairvoyant described Sister Theresa in detail, right down to the brilliant blue color of her eyes. When she told me this, I was astounded. As mentioned earlier, I went to a Catholic school for eight years. The school was run by the Sisters of Mercy order.

Irene continued to tell me that a Chinese man named Chang was my spiritual teacher. Chang had come through many times to help in the delivery of messages to my clients. Finally, Irene began to draw a picture of the spirit she saw in her mind's eye. When I saw Master Chang's warm face, I felt a loving attraction to it. He wore a small cap, sort of a beanie, with an orange top and blue brim. It was the type of cap quite prevalent in China during the early 1900s. He was draped in a long, cobalt blue robe that covered him fully. The robe was accented by an orange mandarin collar with matching orange cuffs. His hands were interlocked within his sleeves. His face was long and narrow, and his eyes were brown and gave a sense of wise gentleness. He wore a traditional Chinese ponytail of the period. The starkness of his bald head was alleviated by a majestic goatee. In the center of his robe near his heart chakra was a golden, ten-pointed star that signified spiritual wisdom. In the middle of the star was a green jewel that represented unconditional love. He was surrounded by the gold light of the highest spiritual realm. This gold light marked Chang as a master.

I was not made aware of his most recent lifetime, or if he ever lived upon the earth. Many times a guide will dress in a style from a period of time that he or she enjoyed the most or that represents a dominant aspect of his or her identification. I could tell by looking at the picture of Chang that he was a soul who had touched the human experience many times. He was truly a master teacher.

I learned about two other guides of mine in a somewhat unorthodox way. As a budding medium, it was important to develop my capabilities on an ongoing basis. So once a week I would sit in a darkened room with six people whom I chose to be with me. Actually, this routine is fairly common among psychics who want to fully develop their extrasensory gifts. During a session in our fourth week of training, I began to feel myself getting extremely tired and fell into a light trance state. This is a state when the conscious mind shuts off and any awareness of our body and our thoughts disappear. It is more common than we think. For instance, many of us are in a trance while engrossed in a television show or reading a book that we can't put down. More commonly, we go into a trance state right before falling asleep.

When I came out of the trance half an hour later, I asked, "What happened?" The group was all excited to inform me of some remarkable results. "An English doctor came through you saying his name is Harry Aldrich," said one person. As they continued, they told me Harry Aldrich was a physician who lived on the northwest side of London. It became apparent that he died in the early 1930s. Someone in the group taped the session, and when I heard the tape, I could hardly recognize my voice. I heard a distinct English accent and a somewhat sober and deliberate manner. To some extent he was dictatorial, but his advice about my health and future sessions with the group was accurate. He said that he chose to return at this time to assist me in my work as a medium.

One of the ways this guide helps me is by amplifying the energy around my physical body during my readings. He is also able to identify physical ailments that my clients may have. Harry Aldrich is a very kind man, but I certainly can feel his distinct authoritarian personality when he comes through.

Some weeks later, we were once again sitting in a circle, and I went into a trance. Once again, another incredible manifestation occurred. When I awakened, my wife said, "You're never gonna believe what happened!"

"What?" I said.

"A man came through by the name of Golden Feather," she said.

"That is an Indian," I replied.

"A North American Indian, to be exact," she continued.

One of the members of the group rewound the tape and played it. I couldn't believe my ears. I could hear the sound of a drum.

"Where did the drum come from?" I asked.

"That's no drum. That's the table in front of us," came the answer.

Earlier that evening, we placed a table in the center of the room. I looked down at the table. I thought it quite amazing that the unique sound of an Indian tom-tom emerged from the very same table.

As I continued to listen to the beating of a drum, there suddenly arose a vociferous sound of an Indian singing in his native language. The tune was beautiful and at the same time spellbinding. After five minutes, the singing ended abruptly. At that point the Indian began to speak: "We are all brothers. You and I are brothers. We come to you and bring you love. Everything is love. You must see love in all things. My name is Golden Feather. I am from the brotherhood. We are with you always. We bring you love. As a sign, we give each one a feather from our headdress to wear as a symbol of our love."

I sat there dumbfounded. It was so real, and yet I could not remember any part of it. I knew it was a special moment, and I was so thrilled that it had been captured on tape and witnessed by others. Since then, our group has sat every Tuesday evening. Occasionally, Golden Feather will come through me with words of love and wonder.

If anything, these experiences make me realize that I am not doing this stuff by myself. I know that indeed there are those spiritual beings, unseen and unknown, who work on our behalf to assist in bringing about changes in our lives. By helping me, my guides are helping all those I touch.

How to Discover Your Own Spirit Guides

I personally never thought about my guides before they appeared to me and other mediums described them to me. I don't think it is necessary to know who your guides are, but some individuals need to know to whom they are speaking. It is a way of rationalizing that someone in spirit is around them and guiding them. It is not enough to know they have teachers, but they want to personalize the connection. This is very understandable. Several techniques can facilitate recognition of spirit guides.

The first step is meditation. (In chapter 11, I explain how to meditate.) You enter meditation with the intent of meeting one of your spiritual guides. When you have reached a sufficiently relaxed state, mentally begin to ask your teacher or teachers to reveal themselves in your mind's eye. If you are relaxed enough and not too anticipatory, you will become aware in your mind's eye of the face of someone or perhaps a part of their clothing. For instance, you might see a feather and recognize this as belonging to an American Indian. At this point you may ask to see more and allow the guide to reveal him/herself to you. Once you have satisfactorily seen a teacher, you may ask to see another. Or you may ask the first one to reveal the lessons you are here to learn. Before coming out of meditation, thank your guide(s). I suggest that you start a journal and write about your guides and any information they reveal to you, especially what their mission is.

This first exercise should be successful, depending on the degree of meditation and relaxation. If you have a difficult time discerning or seeing your teachers, here is another way to receive the same information. As you lie in bed and begin to fall asleep, ask your teacher or teachers to reveal themselves to you in a dream. Repeat the request over and over in your head like a mantra. When you fall asleep, you should dream of your teacher or teachers. Please be patient because the results may not come right away. You may need to repeat your wish each night for a while until you receive results.

·SECTION TWO·

THE SESSIONS

CHAPTER 4

Tragic Transitions

W hen clients walk into my office, I have no prior knowledge of their situation or the reason for the visit. Neither
do I have prior knowledge of events in their lives or whom they
wish to contact. Yet, within an hour, they will have shared with
me some of the most intimate moments of their lives. Their grief,
pain, and greatest desires are revealed as they connect with their
loved ones. Often during this contact a dramatic revelation occurs. A spark of life is relit as they discover their loved ones are
very much alive and communing with them on a daily basis. For
those left on earth, the road ahead begins to clear, as if they were
stepping out of a fog. Somehow they feel that life seems possible
once again.

The Airplane
Many of my clients are extremely distraught and nervous when
they arrive for their sessions. They are grieving their loss, unsure
of what to expect, and nervous about what they might encounter.
These strong emotional vibrations can interfere with the quality of
the communication in much the same way turning on a blow

dryer or vacuum cleaner creates static on a television set. To calm these vibrations and to help synchronize the energies in the room, I often begin a session by guiding my clients through a relaxation meditation. This helps to put their minds at ease and helps me to communicate with spirit people more easily.

Marilyn was noticeably more at peace by the time we finished the meditation. The overwhelming distress I had noted when she entered my office had given way to a calmer receptivity. I welcomed her into my séance room and tried to make her feel as comfortable as possible. As briefly as possible, I explained what she could expect. Almost immediately, I felt a male presence standing to Marilyn's left side.

"Do you know the name Roger?" I questioned.

She replied that Roger was her husband's name.

"I see him with reddish blond hair. He is constantly combing it." As I imitated the combing motion, her eyes began to turn red.

"Oh, yes, he was always fussing with it."

"He is showing me the cockpit of a plane. The dials and arrows on the control panel have ceased to function. I see smoke and fire, then everything goes black. Does this make any sense to you?"

Marilyn started to quiver as she brought out a tissue to dab her eyes.

"Roger died in a plane crash a year ago. His plane went down at night. He was the one I was hoping to contact."

"He says to tell you he loves you very much and has been waiting to speak with you. He is very excited. He wants to wish you a happy anniversary."

She is astonished. "Our anniversary was this past week. My God!"

"Someone is standing next to him whom you know."

Marilyn could not speak.

"It is a little boy. He says his name is Tommy. Do you know him?"

Marilyn was in a frenzy as she practically screamed with excitement, "Yes, oh, yes! Tommy is my son. He was in the plane with Roger. That's how it all started. Tommy wanted Daddy to take him for a ride in the plane."

"He says, 'Mommy, don't be so scared. I'm here with Daddy!' He asks that you please go into his room and take down the *Star Wars* poster from his wall. He doesn't need it anymore."

Marilyn shook her head in disbelief. "That poster is hanging above his bed."

"He is mentioning the name Bobby and wants to tell Bobby something."

"Bobby is my other son," explained Marilyn.

"Tommy says he's not really mad at Bobby for taking his red shirt out of his second drawer and wearing it."

There was a gasp. Once again, Marilyn could not speak. I asked her if she knew what that meant.

"Bobby is wearing the red shirt today. He put it on right before I left."

Marilyn was convinced that she was in contact with her husband and son. Roger continued to provide more information. He mentioned the name of his buddy in the air force and where he was stationed and his duties while in the service.

The sudden loss of a family member can be devastating. The impact is all the more crushing when the passing includes both a spouse and a child through a violent death. These wounds are often very difficult to heal. By the time the session concluded, Marilyn was feeling much lighter. As I walked her out to the car, she said, "James, you have changed my life. I feel like a black cloud has lifted off me. Just knowing that they're all right and they are together makes me feel so much better. Thank you." I told her I was glad that she had gotten the information she needed.

She sat for a moment, then rolled down the window of her car and looked me straight in the eye. "Actually, I'm more than better. I think now I can begin to live again." She was smiling as she pulled away from the curb.

The Drowning

Oftentimes when I sit with a client, the room is filled with the spirits of family or friends who are all attempting to get their thoughts across at once. And just as on the earthly plane, when everyone is speaking at the same time, it is difficult to decipher individual thoughts and from whom they originate. In most cases, if the client has been thinking about someone, it is usually that spirit who will come through first. But in some cases, a spirit pops through as a total surprise to the sitter.

An unexpected spirit usually emerges toward the end of a session. It is comforting to know that even on the other side manners are meaningful. An unexpected spirit will wait until a sitter has reunited with a loved one or until an appropriate opportunity. Frequently, it is an unexpected spirit who has the most compelling message to share with the sitter.

Mark had just finished a wonderful conversation with his father who had passed over several years earlier. In a rather typical session, Mark received answers to the questions he had asked. As the session began to wind down, I felt another presence. I asked him if he knew someone named Doug.

His face went white and he nodded his head wildly up and down. "Yes . . . yes, what is he saying?"

"He says to tell you he will no longer go out into the rain. He is saying to please let his parents know he is okay. Do you understand?"

Mark stammered, "Yes, go on."

"He is talking about getting caught in some sort of a flood and mentions how sorry he is for not realizing how dangerous things were. This is very strange. He is also speaking of having a new bicycle."

"Yes, I understand."

"Did this boy drown? He is giving me a sense of treading swirling water. He shows himself bobbing up and down, and his lungs filling with water."

I could feel pressure on my chest as the sensation of Doug filled my body.

"I have the sense of being dizzy. He begins to lose consciousness and then everything turns black."

"Wow!" exclaimed Mark.

"Do you know if there were fire or rescue people around him? He is showing me that they are standing at the side of the bank."

"Yes, there were many rescue workers who tried to reel him in at several different spots along the river."

I continued. "He is talking about how he tried to grab onto a rope, but he couldn't reach it."

Mark was very somber. "Anything else?"

"He wants you to say hello to Max. Does that make sense?"

"Oh, my God. Max is my son and Doug used to baby-sit him. They became best friends. That's amazing!"

"He is speaking of Florida. He is showing me a baseball cap with something to do with . . . I don't understand this. Hold on. He gives me the thought of Marla or Marlin."

"The Florida Marlins!" yelled Mark. "I just gave Max Doug's Florida Marlins baseball cap. He loves it because it reminds him of Doug."

"He wants him to enjoy it. He also wants Max to say hello to all the kids across the street."

Mark explained that everyone loved Doug. He was a sports nut and all the kids in the neighborhood really liked him.

"Doug is mentioning a new bike again. He loved his new bicycle. I'm not sure why he is going on and on about it," I confessed.

Mark was on the edge of his seat.

"Unbelievable," he finally responded. "In a way, it was the bike that started the whole thing. He got a new bike two days before the storm and rode it down to the riverbank to check out the raging water in the wash. Apparently, the bike got swept up in the rising river. When Doug went after it, he fell in. The water was too strong, and he couldn't get out."

"He wants to give love to Linda."

"Linda is my wife," Mark explained. "I'll tell her hello for him."

"He is very happy you came here and wants you to let everyone know he is doing just great."

"You got it, buddy," Mark grinned, and he tilted his head and looked upward.

A few days later I received a phone call from Doug's family. They were amazed at the detail of information that came through to Mark that no one, not even the television stations, had known. They made an appointment with me, and several weeks later they talked with their son and were reassured of his afterlife. As Doug explained to his parents, his life did not end in that rain-swollen river. He told them that he planned to finish school and even had hopes of having a girlfriend one day. They were happy to know that Doug's life was indeed continuing.

It's Not What You Think

When writing this book, I had to go back through several years of sessions in order to present what I felt were the most common types of personal encounters between loved ones and those who have crossed over the veil of death. In my research, I came across a number of readings that stood out from the rest. Perhaps they were purely unique or included miraculous demonstrations of the powers of spirit, or incredible and surprising facts were revealed during the communication.

I found the following session to be an amazing example of all of the above. It is a story of a couple whose lives were shattered by the death of their son. It was a death that produced more questions than answers. Their son's spirit was very grateful to have had an opportunity to enlighten his parents about the controversial incidents surrounding his death. At the end of the session, not only was he able to restore peace of mind to his parents but, more importantly, his soul was able to finally rest.

Alan and Sandra came to me through the recommendation of friends. They seemed quite skeptical and very unsure of getting themselves involved in something as strange as spiritualism. I gave them my usual introduction, explaining how I received information, and what to expect and what not to. They listened and seemed to understand that they had to be ready for anything.

The first person I picked up in the room was Sandra's mother.

I spoke out. "Sandra, your mother is here. She is very close to you and says to be careful of that kitchen knife."

"Oh, my God," replied Sandra. "I was sharpening it today and almost cut my finger. Was she watching me?"

I said, "It had to be your mother because I wasn't in your kitchen."

Sandra smiled, and her mother continued sending me thoughts.

"Your mother says she likes the new patio furniture."

"Yes, that's right. We just bought some the other day at Sears. She used to sit outside on the porch a lot when she lived with us."

"She has a great sense of humor. She says she was sitting there waiting to die."

Suddenly, I was interrupted with the thoughts of another spirit who was emphatic about being heard.

"Yes, I hear you," I told the spirit. "There is someone else with your mother, Sandra. It is a young man who passed over very quickly. Your mother says you've been asking for him."

The couple's eyes began to well up with tears, but I went ahead.

"Do you understand the name of Steven?"

They both turned pale and began to cry. They acknowledged that Steven was their son, and the reason they came to see me.

I continued. "Steven is very agitated. He doesn't feel at rest. He has been trying to get through to you for a while. Has he been over there about two years?"

"No, just about ten months, closer to a year."

"Hmmm. He says his death really destroyed you. He is so sorry about his death. He has tried to right a wrong. I don't know what he is talking about. Do you understand what he means?"

Alan spoke up. "Yes, I think so. What else is he saying?"

"Gee, he gives me a burning sensation. I feel like my head has been blown to bits. I'm sorry, but this is what he is giving me. Was he shot with a gun?"

"Yes."

"He says you found him in his bedroom."

"That's right." They both wiped their eyes.

"I am sorry to bring you this information, but I believe your son was on drugs, or at least experimented with them."

"Yes, we found that out," said Sandra

"Your son is very strong. He is yelling—it was Ronnie! Who is Ronnie?"

"Ronnie was a friend of his."

I then transmitted information that changed the entire feeling in the room, not only for the couple but for myself as well.

"His watch. He is talking about his gold watch."

Alan said, "We couldn't find it after he died. We looked everywhere."

"Your son gave it to Ronnie for payment. Ronnie was angry. Do you know if there was some kind of fight before your son died?"

"No."

"Steven is screaming at me, I didn't kill myself. It was Ronnie. Ronnie did it to me. I didn't kill myself!"

There was a dead-calm silence. None of us could believe what just came through. Very rarely will a spirit come through with the name of its murderer. In this case, Steven wanted justice. I sat back and tried to gain composure before continuing.

"Steven is saying something about suicide. Did you think he committed suicide?"

They both acknowledged that they did.

"Your son is trying to let you know it wasn't suicide. He wouldn't do that. Do you know if the police questioned his death?"

"No, we all thought Steven killed himself because he was on drugs. They found drugs in his body," said Sandra.

"I am getting very clearly that your son and this Ronnie person were in a fight. Ronnie wanted some money and drugs. Alan, do you own a pistol, a small gun?"

"Yes, that is the one he used."

"He tells me he got it from a bottom dresser drawer? Is this correct?"

"Jesus, how the hell would you know that? Yeah, that's right."

"Do you know if this Ronnie had a prior police record?"

"No, we don't think so," stated Sandra.

"Your son keeps showing me a struggle about money. Steven owed Ronnie money. This guy was really screwed up at the time. He was very high on something. This is Ronnie I am speaking about. Listen, your son keeps showing me a garage. It is a brick garage with a white door. It has three small windows. He opens it and goes to the left, side wall."

"We don't have a garage. What does it mean?"

"I don't know, but keep it, please. It might make sense later on. Your boy is happy that he told you about this. He says you will understand it one day. Get Ronnie. He mentions a name—Sharon or Sherry."

Alan spoke up, "That's his sister."

"Did she just have a baby?"

"No."

"Well, I don't know what it means, just keep the information and see if it makes sense later on. Your mother is jumping in here and telling me you helped Steven. He is all right."

"Thank you."

"She is also showing me something to do with peeling potatoes."

Sandra replied. "Yesterday, I made potato soup—it was Mom's recipe. I thought of her."

"She tells me it turned out well."

With that, they both smiled. The session continued for a little bit longer. Steven spoke about his funeral and how he wished his mother hadn't gone through so much trouble over his headstone. The meeting ended, and we said good-bye. The couple were convinced they made contact with their son. They told me they would listen to the tape once again and see if they could make any sense out of the incredible information.

Several months later, I received a phone call from Sandra. She wanted to tell me how grateful the family was for all my help, and to inform me that several things had occurred in the interim. They called the police and spoke with a detective who knew of their son's death. The detective followed up by investigating the story about Ronnie. When he visited Ronnie's house, he found the brick garage with three windows. On the left side in a wall panel was a kilo of heroin, assorted drugs, and Steven's gold watch. The detective took Ronnie into custody. After being questioned by the police, Ronnie finally admitted that Steven had owed him some money for a drug deal and hadn't paid up. Steven offered his gold watch, which Ronnie took, but Ronnie still wanted the money. The day that Ronnie came to collect it, Steven took his father's gun out of the drawer to protect himself. When Steven told Ronnie he didn't have the rest of the money, Ronnie grabbed the gun and shot Steven in the head. Ronnie admitted that he was high at the time. Ronnie was brought to trial and is currently serving a life sentence in a state penitentiary.

The Marine

People pass from this life in a variety of ways. Some pass quietly in their sleep, others initiate it themselves, and still others are involved in an accident of some kind. Although we choose our way of death long before we enter the earth plane, none seems more tragic than a violent transition. At least it seems to have the most impact on those of us still in physical form.

In many cases, a person who leaves violently or quickly is unaware that the death process has taken place. Because the trauma occurs so fast, the spirit body may be literally thrown out of the physical body. The spirit may remain unaware of its predicament for many years to come. During that time, a spirit may visit all the familiar places of its earth life and may believe it is still alive, albeit dreaming. This spirit phenomenon is termed *lost soul* or, as many of us call it, a *ghost*. If a spirit is disturbed, unhappy, or restless, we categorize it as a *poltergeist*. Fortunately, many spirits on the other side are involved in rescuing these lost and misguided souls.

In certain circumstances where there are bothersome spirits, there are several ways to deal with them. Remember, they only have as much strength and control as you let them. You are in charge and need to know that at all times. In the majority of poltergeist cases, a spirit does not realize it has passed over, so you begin with this idea. Also, each spirit has a different set of circumstances surrounding its death. I would advise going to the area of the house most affected by the disturbance. The time involved in removing this energy varies with each case. Before you begin, I advise you to do a ritual of personal protection and ask your spirit guides or guardian angels to be with you and assist you. This should always be done prior to any intuitive work.

The first thing to do is to create an atmosphere in the house or room by raising the vibrations in that particular area. This is accomplished by playing spiritual or religious music such as a setting of the *Our Father*, or *Ave Maria*, or any hymn, song, or music of a high spiritual vibration. Next, purify the affected area by cleansing the atmosphere around it. Burning sage in the room accomplishes this nicely. Other scents that are equally effective are frankincense and myrrh. These three aromas are sensitive to extremely high frequencies and help to clear out dark energies. Thirdly, bring as much natural light into the area as possible. Raise the blinds and open the curtains. Finally, it is important to meditate in an attempt to reach the disturbed spirit. It does not matter if you see it or feel it. Let it know that it has passed into another dimension and tell it to ask for a parent or grandparent to guide it into the next dimension. Remind the troubled spirit over and over again that it does not need to stay on the earth side of the veil, and that indeed it will be in a much happier place on the spiritual side where it will no longer feel enslaved. Please make sure you send these thoughts to a spirit with love and compassion. Depending on the severity of the situation, a cleansing might take a few days or even weeks.

There are also many situations where a person passes violently, as in the case of a murder. This spirit usually becomes aware of its predicament after a brief period of adjustment. Usually, the spirit is met by a relative or a guide right away. The following session offers a unique perspective of a spirit as he describes the realization of his own death.

Before I continue, it is important that I point out that whenever I do a reading I tell a sitter everything that comes through my mind. I have an agreement with the spirit world that if they provide me with the information, then it is appropriate for me to tell all to the individual for whom I am reading. I do this because I am just the medium. It is not my job to censor any of the given information. Besides, there might be a particular fact that the sitter might not understand if I did not tell everything. Therefore, I describe, as vividly as I am given, the visual details and scenes, including colors, and any feelings, whether joyful or uncomfortable.

A young man came into my office on the recommendation of a friend. I knew nothing about this man and did not understand the immediate urge I felt from the other side. Someone was anxious to speak, and so I began.

"There seems to be a lot of separation, from your family. Are you away from your family? I mean, do they live in another state?"

"Yes," came the reply.

"Does the name Laura mean anything to you?"

"Yes, she is my sister; she lives in Arizona."

"I don't know why, but I do want to stay within the family vibration. Are there three kids in the family, two boys and a girl?"

"Yeah . . . well, there was."

"Yes, because I am getting a very strong sensation of a young man here. I think he is your brother. Is that right?"

"That's who I've been thinking about."

"He gives me the name Mike. Does that make sense?"

The young man began to warm up. "Yes, yes, that's him. That's his name."

"He is saying he is okay. He is very happy you came here today. He wants you to tell your mom and dad he is all right. He is mentioning Texas."

"Texas is where my parents live. It is where we were raised. How is he doing?"

"He is fine. He can't believe I can hear him. He's wanted to do this for so long. He has met some friends in the spirit world. From the military. His buddies. Do you understand?"

"Yes, I do. Please, go on."

"Was he in Vietnam? Because he is talking very quickly about the war. The war in Vietnam. He says he has reunited with his buddies from the corps in 'Nam. He didn't want to go there."

"That's right! I was young at the time, but my mom has told me how Mike didn't want to go."

"He seems to pass rather quickly."

I felt myself falling into a deeper trance. I was being visually thrown into a world of fire and pain. I was in the middle of Vietnam. It seemed as if the world were going crazy. Bright, burning colors of yellow and orange surrounded me. In front of me I sensed a loud "pop." I stared at my client and explained that I had to stop for a minute. I asked my guides to remove this death memory experience; it was affecting my physical body too much. The guides quickly took it away. The scene began to play out again, but this time I was an observer.

"I am being shown a man in the brush. It is very dark. The man who I believe is your brother looks quite nervous. He is walking with the rest of his troop. He tries to take off his coat, but the bottom of his coat seems to get snagged on something around his belt."

The young man tried without success to hold back his tears. He could tell that I was reliving the scene of his brother's death. I saw the very top part of a grenade being ripped from its place by the zipper of the coat. The force of rushing air exploded through the soldier's body, and he was decapitated. The scene went black.

I stared at my client.

"Did your brother get blown up by a grenade that got caught in his clothing?"

The young man slumped back into his chair. His mouth worked slowly, trying to form the correct words.

"Yes, that is what it said on the document sent by the government."

I couldn't believe it. I had never had anyone come across so vividly. It was difficult to contain my excitement as I continued.

"That's amazing! Your brother is a fantastic communicator. Hold on, let's see what else he wants to say. He is describing what it felt like when he woke up. He says that after what seemed like a couple of seconds, he came back to consciousness. He looked around and noticed he felt very different, not as fatigued as he had been. He saw a group of his buddies standing in a circle screaming, but he couldn't hear their words until he moved in closer. They were screaming out his name. Mike! Mike! He answered, but they could not hear him. He walked over to the circle and noticed they were looking down at the remaining pieces of a human carcass. Suddenly, he had a very strange and eerie sensation through his body. He looked down at the dog tags his platoon buddy was holding. His saw his name on them."

The young man was fascinated. "That's unreal. He actually knew what was going on."

"He says he was a bit confused but realized he must be dead. He is describing a very strong sensation of peace and calmness. Hold on . . . He wants me to tell you he was greeted by Alice. Did he know an Alice?"

"Alice is our grandmother."

"Well, Alice came to help him over. He was shocked and, at the same time, happy and relieved. He says she was standing next to him. He wants me to tell you he has seen Pappy also, and he still has Jo Jo with him."

"Pappy was my grandfather and Jo Jo was his German shepherd. Mike and Jo Jo were always together. This is incredible. So, animals also live on?"

"All living creatures live on. Your brother wants me to tell you how very sorry he is for causing so much worry and heartache. Please realize he is all right and living a full life."

"He doesn't have to worry about that. Just let him know we love him very much, and we're happy he is around us. We look forward to seeing him again one day."

"He says he and everyone else over there . . . he's laughing . . . , including Jo Jo, will be waiting."

When an animal comes through during a reading as in this last case, a client usually looks at me somewhat perplexed. We don't think of little Fluffy or Rover surviving death. But why not? Animals are made of the same God-given life force as humans. When an animal comes through, the vibration is similar to reading a human. An animal's personality traits (animals do have them) come across clearly to me. Many times an animal will express how it loved a particular food or how it liked to sit on a particular chair. Like its human counterpart, an animal will on occasion describe in detail how it died, or how it had a difficult time swallowing food when it was sick, or how it was hard to walk at the end.

The following is a beautiful story from a reading by an English medium who has since passed. I believe it encompasses the true meaning of how animals love us unconditionally.

Once upon a time, there was a simple farmer who lived in England. As sometimes happens, hard times took away his farm, and eventually everyone in his family died. The only thing left in his life was his old, white, swayback nag horse named Patty whom he helped bring into the world. Patty and the farmer stayed together many, many years until the day arrived when it was the horse's turn to pass. The farmer, left completely alone, was totally distraught. Years later, when it was the farmer's turn to pass, he woke up in spirit and found himself sitting in a beautiful meadow. He didn't know where he was and thought perhaps he was dreaming. He stared at a hill that stood in the distance. Suddenly, a horse came galloping over the hill toward him. It was his old nag Patty, but she was not the old, arthritic, swayback horse he remembered. Instead, she was a brilliant, young, and vigorous mare. As the horse drew closer, the farmer indeed recognized his Patty and felt her love. It was Patty's love that guided the farmer into the spirit world.

The bonds of love between ourselves and our pets live on as we journey to the other side. Love bonds, no matter with whom, always continue.

CHAPTER 5

Fatal Collisions

One day we will all return to our spiritual home, of that we can be assured. However, the manner of how we leave this earth and where we arrive varies with each individual. Many leave the body unexpectedly and tragically, as Mike did in Vietnam. Unfortunately, many more people die in car accidents. As an intermediary between the spiritual and earth worlds, I have been impressed with many thoughts of those who have passed by accidents. Why this occurs needs to be explained.

First, there are *no* accidents. Such incidents are the direct results of the spiritual law of cause and effect, or karma. Let me describe what I mean: A person goes to a party and makes a conscious decision to drink alcohol. After he is sufficiently intoxicated, he decides to call it a night and drive home. At the same time, a couple are returning home after seeing a movie. The inebriated individual's vision is blurred, and he does not see the oncoming car until too late. Unfortunately, he rams right into the couple, and they die instantly.

In this scenario, the death is a result or effect of this man's decision to drink. His intoxicated impairment is the cause of the accident, and he is responsible for ending two people's lives. This is a karmic situation. A balance will have to be played out in another lifetime because the couple have died. In other words, all our actions are repaid in kind, positively or negatively, in this life or another lifetime. The law of cause and effect is a natural, immutable law of the universe, and there is a resolution to every experience by way of karmic action or the grace of God.

What appears as an accident, or even a natural disaster, is not always what it seems. Nothing happens by chance. Not only are things based on karmic obligations, but a soul, or a group of souls, makes an agreement in spirit before entering the physical world. Everything in life occurs as part of a spiritual plan. All of life is about learning from our experiences. In order to learn the fullness of life, each soul has to experience it all. Therefore, along with the positive, a soul must go through a negative experience. One must learn the duality of nature. It is through the negative that the positive is appreciated.

With this in mind, certain souls agree in spirit to experience a natural disaster, or a plane crash, and agree to leave their bodies in this manner. Is this a conscious decision? No, I don't believe it could be. Our egos would not allow this type of harm to our bodies. Another way to look at disasters and accidents is this: These souls may be finishing past karma from another lifetime. Then, too, is the question: Was this accident or disaster in some way a help to others? In other words, how were family and close friends affected by this person's death? Will they have a clearer insight into love and an appreciation of life? Will the passing of a loved one be valuable to them in their spiritual growth? We cannot understand these things with our rational minds because these matters are of a spiritual nature. Suffice it to say that our lives are part of a much bigger picture than we can fathom.

Often, clients ask if a loved one felt pain at the time of a fatal impact. In most cases, a spirit blacks out and does not remember. Spirits frequently comment that they see the crushed vehicle and wonder what poor person has been killed. Not until they recognize their own lifeless form do they realize that they have suffered the experience.

When spirits first realize their own death, they may be quite upset, to say the least, especially if they still feel very much alive. When death by accident occurs, and a spirit is literally thrown out of its body, a relative, good friend, or guide will usually be nearby to assist the newcomer through the death transition. The newcomer soon understands that there is life in spirit form. It looks down at its spirit body and realizes it looks identical to its former physical body. Sometimes a spirit may wake up in a hospital, which is not the same as a hospital on earth, and be greeted by a relative or dear friend who welcomes the spirit and informs it of its passing by way of an accident.

One must realize that with any death, especially a sudden one, a spirit might need further help and understanding to acclimatize itself to a new environment. Thank God there are those beautiful souls who assist them. On earth we would refer to these souls as social workers or therapists because, like them, spiritual helpers mentally assist the newly arrived into an unfamiliar environment.

When I work with bereaved parents, they often say that the loss of a child is the worst experience one can ever have in life. No one is ever prepared for a child's death. The grieving parents inevitably blame themselves for the child's death, as if they were responsible or able to prevent it. But only God has that power.

As you will see in the following reading, a child tries to reassure his mother that he is fine and that she should not feel responsible for his death. By words of love, laughter, and intimate information, a child seeks to comfort his mother. When the reading was over, I noticed a complete change in the mother. She was no longer crying.

Boy on the Motorcycle

This particular reading occurred at the home of a sitter. Eight people were in the group. I had never met the people there, nor had I known anything about those they wanted to contact.

After three readings, I suddenly turned my head to the left

side of the room and noticed a lady sitting on the couch. She was crying.

"May I come to you?" I asked.

She looked over and hesitantly replied, "Yes, that's fine."

"There is a young blond man who has been sitting on the couch with you all night. Is this someone you recognize?"

"Yes, I believe so."

"He tells me his name is Stephen. Do you understand the name?"

The woman breaks down in tears and exclaims, "Yes, yes, I do. He is my son."

I continued. "He seems to have an excellent sense of humor and a hearty laugh. Does this make sense?"

"Yes, that's right."

"His sense of humor is dry and a bit cutting, if you know what I mean?"

The woman shakes her head in the affirmative. She smiles slightly as she becomes aware that she is really communicating with her son.

"He says hello to Diane, and something about her knowing about a party?"

"Diane was his girlfriend."

The woman thought about the reference to a party and could not make a connection. Suddenly, she exclaimed, "Oh, my God! Diane was at a party with him the night he died. They were at a friend's party."

"He is showing me a motorcycle on a slippery road. Do you understand?"

"Yes," she replied.

"He goes around a bend very quickly and then down a hill. Hmmm . . . you know, he was a little bit tipsy when he was on this motorcycle."

The woman continues to nod her head as she listens.

"What does 'Greenleaf' mean, please? He shows me a sign with this name on it."

The woman replied, "That is the name of the street where he had the accident."

"I see. He is now showing me a dark blue car. Did his motorcycle skid into this blue vehicle?"

"Yes, it did. Stephen was thrown from the bike and went under the car." She breaks down.

"Stephen wants you to know he loved the yearbook picture of himself with the beautiful inscription underneath it."

"That's right. We actually have a copy of it hanging in the living room."

"He wants you to know something very important. He says you have been carrying around a lot of guilt for his death, and that is wrong. You were not responsible."

"Well, if I had called him that night, he might not have gone to that party."

"Stephen says he would have gone anyway, you know that. He always did what he wanted."

"Yes, he did," the woman replied. "He's right. I guess there was no way of my preventing the accident. I just feel so bad that there was nothing I could do."

"Yes, but do you understand it wasn't your fault?"

"Yes, I see now, thank you." She bowed her head and continued listening to the rest of the reading.

Stephen mentioned several evidential items that his mother knew his father and sister would recognize.

Up until that point it was a standard reading. The information that followed was both intriguing and quite incredible. Stephen turned out to be a medium's best friend. He was a great communicator and was able to describe details through a fun-loving personality.

"Stephen says to say hello to all his friends. God, he had a lot!"

"Yes, he did."

"Do you know if his friends had their own funeral service for him?" I asked.

"No, I don't think so. I mean . . . they put flowers at the accident sight, but I don't think . . ."

"He is showing me the initials J. D., and someone giving a toast. I don't know what the heck it means."

The woman started to laugh, and screamed out, "Oh, yes, some of his buddies climbed over the fence of the cemetery and left a Jack Daniel's bottle on top of his grave. I guess you can call it sort of a service."

Everyone in the room laughed and then went over and gave this woman a hug. Stephen assured her that he would be around all the time and "to be cool" with it all. His mother looked toward the ceiling and started to talk to Stephen herself. Not only was she able to accept his death, but she was free of the irrational guilt. She was also happy to know that her son was still seeing her every move.

The Cheerleader

Just like on the earth, when certain things bother us, we feel we need resolution. In spirit, we are the same. When we pass over to the spirit world, we exist based on thoughts and actions of our earth life. If we did something of which we were ashamed when we were in physical form, our negative feeling or condition might stay within our consciousness for a long time.

If we die with unresolved issues, we cannot rest peacefully or spiritually progress until our earthly issues have been resolved. One of the rewards of doing my work is helping a spirit seek and receive forgiveness for some wrongdoing. A spirit is then free of its negative tie and can move forward in its growth on the other side of life.

As I mentioned previously, many times I will bring in unexpected spirits. When this is the case, there is something very important a spirit needs to convey to a client. In the following instance, a spirit is an old high school friend who wants forgiveness for past actions.

During a group meeting late one Saturday evening, just before I was about to close the session, I was directed to two women and a man sitting across from me on the couch. I knew somehow they were all linked together. I directed my questioning to the woman in the middle.

"Excuse me, may I come to you?"

"Yes," she replied.

"There is a young woman here about your age. She feels to me to be a bit disturbed about something, like something is worrying her. Do you know the name of Stacey?"

"Yes, I went to school with her."

"She died in a very sudden manner. She is showing me glass and blood and then points to her head. She was not prepared for her death. Does this make sense?"

"Yes, yes, it does. I was thinking about her while sitting here."

"She says she wouldn't miss this for the world. I must tell you, I think Stacey was a party girl."

"Yes, she was."

"I get a feeling that she was very popular at school, and the number one guest on the party circuit."

Everyone began to laugh.

"Before she died, her head felt very fuzzy as if she was drugged or drunk. I see her in a car. There was an impact to her head. I see lots of glass and blood. I think she was in a car accident, and I'm sorry to say, but I do feel she went through the windshield."

Both girls began to cry out, "That is right."

"She tells me this happened at an intersection. She was at a party, and she says she got pretty 'fucked-up.' "

"Yes."

"She tells me she knows both of you. Is that correct?"

"Yes it is. We all went to school together."

I now directed my questions to Julie, the other woman on the couch.

"She is showing me a picture of the three of you. Do you have the picture she is referring to?"

"Yeah, I was just looking at it."

"This is weird. Now, she is showing me something like sports outfits. I'm not sure if they are for football or something to do with varsity. She shows me a letter on a sweater."

Julie responded. "We were all cheerleaders together in school. I was looking at a picture of us as cheerleaders. The three of us were wearing our uniforms. The uniforms have a letter in the middle."

I wiped my brow and breathed a sigh of relief. I was happy that they understood the information.

I continued. "She always wanted to be a mother."

"That's right. She would talk about having a family, and all the things they would do together."

"She wants me to tell you that she is taking care of children where she is. She is like a social worker, and she loves it."

The two women nodded their heads and smiled. Suddenly, Stacey's mood began to change.

"This is very strange. She is giving me a sense of heaviness and is beginning to cry. She is very upset about how she treated both of you. She is telling me—forgive my French—that she was a bitch to you guys."

They both shook their heads yes.

"She tells me that she broke off her friendship with you because she wanted to be with friends who were more popular at school and connected to the 'in' crowd. She says that she was a jealous person and started arguments between people. She always wanted to be the center of attention. Did you gals stop speaking to her for a while?"

"Yeah, that's right. We didn't speak to her for the few months before she died."

"She wants me to tell you she is very sorry. She was wrong, and is asking you to please forgive her for how she behaved. She says she was always so obsessed with being the most popular person in school that she overlooked the feelings of others. It was a stupid thing to do."

The girls began to cry.

"Will you please forgive her? She has been very bothered by the way she has behaved."

"Yes, of course we do," said Julie.

"She wants you to know she feels your hurt. She has experienced her own treatment of you and hates what she did."

The girls wiped their tears.

"Julie, did you and the young man next to you get married over the summer?"

"Yes, in August."

"Did you think that it would have been nice to have Stacey as one of your bridesmaids?"

"Yes. We were both thinking of that. That is so weird."

"She is showing me a pink dress, and her hair tied up in a pink ribbon."

Julie yelled out, "Oh, my God, pink was the color of the bridesmaids' dresses. Everyone had a pink ribbon in her hair."

I went on. "Stacey says to tell you that she was a part of your wedding in spirit. She says, 'Did you think you could have a party without me around?' "

With that remark, everyone laughed and thanked Stacey for coming. Stacey, in turn, thanked her friends for their undying love and forgiveness. At that moment, I saw Stacey go over and hug each girl, then turn around and smile at me as an acknowledgment of her gratitude. Slowly, she disappeared into the ethers. The group took a couple of minutes to acknowledge the incredible experience and the feeling of peace and love they all felt.

It is important to understand that we continue to have opportunities to change our attitudes and behavior once we leave our physical bodies. If someone was mean and unkind when alive, as Stacey admitted, that person may have a new awareness of herself on the other side. She saw how she misbehaved on the earth and also realized that she was given many opportunities on earth to convey love, but instead she chose to be troublesome. With this realization comes understanding and a wish to be forgiven.

The most common request from the spirit people in most of my readings is one of forgiveness. It is not only healing for the spirit to be sorry for earthly wrongdoing, but it is an inspiration to those still on earth to begin to resolve any problems or upsets with other people. Spirit people want us to start living a life free of judgment and prejudice. The spirits express over and over again that *love and forgiveness* is the *only* way!

The Policeman

One of the most commonly asked questions is: *If spirits can see events before they occur, why don't they tell us what to expect?* One must understand that spirit people can only tell us what they know and only what is spiritually correct to report. Although a spirit has attained a keener sense of awareness and an expanded consciousness, it can give information *only* from the level of its enlightenment.

Let me explain further. Earth is our schoolroom. We come here to learn various lessons, and these lessons vary for every person. Each of us incarnates at a different level of growth, and each needs to go through different experiences in order to gain wisdom and expand our awareness of the bigger picture of life. As Jesus said, "In my father's house are many mansions." This means that there are various spiritual levels of existence. When we die, we enter a spiritual level that matches the thoughts and deeds of our earthly life. A spirit can give us knowledge only from the spiritual level it has attained.

Moreover, in the spirit world, spirit people respect and adhere to spiritual laws. If they defy these laws, they would be going against the natural state of harmony and balance and would not be able to spiritually evolve. So instead of giving us answers to what might happen, they abide by spiritual law and allow us to make our own choices.

As an example, if someone asks his deceased mother a question regarding whether or not he will marry, there are two possible responses. First, the mother might be aware of the requested information and impress my mind with an answer. On the other hand, if a marriage is a karmic lesson for her child, the mother will not want to compromise the child's spiritual growth by giving an answer to an upcoming karmic test. An individual *must* go through the human experience alone. Even with our guides and angels, we must make our own decisions based upon our own awareness. One could say that each of us is constantly being *put to the test.*

The following reading is a wonderful example of how a spirit might not be aware of something in earthly life but is now able to see certain details of a future event. Let me stress that this is usually *not* the case, but as you will see, it is amazing when it occurs. This session took place within a group setting. I went to a lady in the room and tuned into her grandmother, who was standing right next to her. The grandmother came through with strong evidential information; she related how she died and commented on some new pillows on her granddaughter's couch. I thought it was a complete reading until something very strange happened.

"Carla, do you know someone on the earth by the name of Joanne?"

She began to think and could not recall anyone in her life with that name. So I continued.

"Well, there seems to be a man standing next to me who insists you do."

She still could not recall anyone.

"He talks about a motorcycle accident. He died in a motorcycle crash, and he says it was on his way home from work."

She continued to think, and then suddenly her face turned white. She screamed out.

"Oh, my God, I think so."

"He is mentioning the name of Kathy?"

"Yes. My best friend's name is Kathy, and Paul is her husband. He died in a motorcycle crash."

Carla began to get very excited, and we had to stop for a couple of minutes for her to gain control. Then, I continued.

"Paul shows me a uniform, a police uniform. He also shows me a parade of police cars—it appears they are in some type of procession."

"Yes, they did that for his funeral."

"I see several policemen carrying his coffin. Do you know if his grave site is near some kind of a wall?"

"I don't remember . . . no, I don't really know. I'll have to ask Kathy."

"Would you know if Kathy has hung a plaque on the wall with Paul's badge, which includes his picture?"

"I don't know."

"Please ask. He says that he saw her standing in front of the plaque and talking to him."

"Okay, I'll ask."

It was then that Paul began to give out information that was incredible and completely unexpected. Not always knowing how to interpret what I receive, I didn't understand the information at all.

"Paul says he has seen the baby. He knows of the baby. He refers to a baby girl and says he was there when she was born. Do you understand this?"

Carla had a blank look on her face. Then she began to cry and put her hand to her mouth. She began to speak, sobbing between words.

"Yes, yes . . . I understand. When Paul was killed, Kathy was two months pregnant, but he didn't know. Kathy had the baby five months ago. Her name is Joanne."

Everyone in the room, including me, let out a gasp.

Later, Carla learned that Paul was indeed buried next to a wall—on the side of a mausoleum. Kathy had framed Paul's badge, and it, along with his picture, hung in the living room. Kathy told Carla that she had been standing in front of her husband's picture asking for a sign from Paul that he was all right. She was pleased to hear the results of the reading.

To this day, Kathy feels reassured to know that her lovely husband is not only alive on the other side but that he is watching over their little baby girl from heaven.

My Mother and the Bus

The following session occurred at a benefit for AIDS Project Los Angeles in 1992. I was invited to do an open demonstration for the public as an opportunity to view death from a somewhat unorthodox perspective. Because a public demonstration can consist of upwards of five hundred people, there has to be a way for me to make a link between the spirit world and earthly participants. This is accomplished by my spirit guides, who learn of a spirit's situation and very carefully position the spirit behind me. I have *no* say in the positioning or order in which I receive the information and never know who will appear.

During my fourth reading, a female spirit began to speak to me.

"There is a lady here, and she is telling me that she died in Mexico. Does this make sense to anyone in the room?"

There was no response, so I continued.

"This woman is telling me she was in a car accident, and it involved a bus. Yes, I believe she crashed into a bus. Does that make sense to anyone here?"

Again there was no response. It is rare when someone in the room does not recognize the information. When it does occur, I find out later that someone in the audience recognized the information, but either the person is too shocked by its accuracy and does not want to be exposed in a public forum, or the information cannot be interpreted correctly until the event is over.

It was the latter that occurred on that evening. After a two-hour demonstration, I said my good-byes, and as I was packing my things to leave, a dark-haired man introduced himself.

"Excuse me, my name is Ed Auger."

"Hi, can I help you?" I replied.

"I was just wondering if the information about the lady in Mexico could have been for me. My mom died in a car accident in Mexico, but it wasn't with a bus. It was with a truck."

I told him, "No, this lady was clearly showing me a bus. The bus had some kind of writing on its side. Are you sure it was a truck?"

"Yeah, I think so, but I'll check with my dad. Thanks a lot."

With that, we left the room and went our separate ways. A month later I received an urgent phone call from Ed. He told me that he had spoken to his father in Mexico, who confirmed that his mother's accident occurred with a bus. He even sent Ed a copy of the newspaper clipping of the event. Ed was very distraught that he didn't recognize the information the first time and hoped his mother wasn't upset with him. He told me the reason he wasn't sure of the information was that at the time of the accident he was only two years old. We arranged an appointment in the hope that Ed could have a reunion with the mother he barely knew.

"Ed, your mother was a very pretty woman. She had beautiful brown eyes and dark brown hair. I see her pulling it back."

"I only have one picture of her and that is what she looks like," Ed responded.

"Well, your mom is disagreeing with you. She insists you have another picture of her in your living room."

"No, not that I can think of."

"She says it isn't a regular picture. There is something special about it. Funny, she mentions it was taken right before she married your father. Do you know something about a painting of her?"

"Oh, God, yes. I have a portrait of my mother when she was nineteen hanging in my living room. It was right after she met my dad."

"She is laughing. She says you are so finicky about everything in that living room. She is also showing me some sort of masks. Tribal, I believe."

"Yes, they are hanging on the opposite wall of her painting. I collect African masks. That's amazing!"

"She is talking about your dad. She says something about him having some medal. Let me get this straight, hold on. Okay, does your dad have any kind of award, a medal on a ribbon?"

Ed was not sure.

"Your mother was from a very well respected family. I think they were well known in a political sense. Does this sound right to you?"

"Yes, exactly. In Mexico, her father was equivalent to a mayor. He was very high up and influential."

"She is also trying to give me her name. She gives me it in three separate words. Spanish. One of them sounds like Camille or Camilla?"

"Unbelievable. Her name was Camilla Dolores Garda."

"Oh, good. That's really good. Your mother is a very good communicator."

There was a pause for a few minutes.

"I'm sorry to say this, but I must give you exactly what I get. I don't censor anything."

"No, that's all right, go ahead."

"Do you know if your mother had to get married?"

"What do you mean?"

"Well, she is saying something about being forced into marriage."

Ed was in shock. He never heard this before and found it hard to believe. I told him that I might not be interpreting it right myself and to ask his father. The reading continued for some time. His mother mentioned a diamond ring and spoke of Ed's work in the financial world, and his recent move.

Ed left the meeting pleased but still puzzled. A few days later he called and said that he spoke to his father about the meeting. His father confirmed a medal, one he received in the military. He said he keeps it in a bedroom drawer next to the diamond ring he gave his wife.

Ed then explained the message regarding his mother being forced to get married. It turned out that Ed's father remarried two years after his mother died. Ed's father told Ed that he had to marry this woman because she became pregnant, and it would ruin his family's reputation if he didn't. His father never told anyone and always kept that fact a family secret.

Ed was positive that he had been communicating with his mother. He was happy to know that she is always with him and will be waiting when it is his turn to return home to the spirit world. He said he looks forward to the time when they will be reunited and together forever.

CHAPTER 6

AIDS

Throughout recorded history, each generation has been challenged with a devastating plague of one type or another. It is unfortunate that I have to write a chapter devoted to the subject, but AIDS has become commonplace in today's society. It has taken its position among cancer and heart disease as a killer of the masses. Often I have been asked: *Why does AIDS exist? What must we learn from it?* Hundreds of books have been written attempting to unravel these questions. I am not one to profess a wealth of knowledge on the subject, nor would I attempt to give an explanation in this book for its existence. I believe the reasons are too complex, and there are no simple answers to these questions. I can only relay to the reader my experience of this disease from a spiritual point of view—from those who have crossed the threshold of death and have explained why they personally had to go through the AIDS experience.

Let me reiterate one point. *All* things are created from universal thought. Even though we do not see thought, it exists. I have pointed out earlier that there is a universal law of cause and effect that is constant, much like the movement of energy that animates our world. In other words, it is our thinking that creates the conditions of our lives. Very few of us live the truth of who we are. Instead, we misuse the power of our own thoughts. Even those who preach truth seem unable to live up to their godly philosophy. So instead of using our thoughts to share the ideals of an unconditional loving God, we turn our energy to bigotry and prejudice.

Too many people seem preoccupied with playing God on earth. Some use their material power to take control and dominate others. Only the ego is greedy for self-serving power, and it can find it anywhere—in a corporate boardroom, or in a government committee room, or on a church pulpit. Alongside of power is the belief that a certain amount of material wealth makes us special or valuable. We all are aware that some of us have profited and still profit by the exploitation of other human beings. Ultimately, it is up to us as individuals to know that our worth and value cannot be measured by any amount of money that we may have in the bank, or the size of our house, or the number of cars we own. When we pass on to the other side, the only question we will be asked has to do with the *amount of love* we have in our hearts.

We are *all* the same. God has *not* chosen one group above another. When we dare to be aware, we will raise our understanding and compassion and see everyone as part of the universal energy of God. We will be free of prejudice and hatred based on someone's color, race, sex, or gender preference. God is not limited. Only humans limit their thinking. I personally believe that by spreading hatred, prejudice, and intolerance we have contributed to the spread of AIDS. It is our wrong way of thinking that causes a general feeling of malaise and lack of harmony that our world finds itself in today.

People often ask if there is a cure for AIDS. I tell them: *Yes.* There is a cure for every type of malady that afflicts us, but no cure will be found until we begin to shift our consciousness away from self-serving attitudes and begin to appreciate and love each other.

The condition known as AIDS, although a horrendous disease, has also been an incredible opportunity for growth and enlightenment. Previously associated with gay men, it has now reached the general population. People throughout this planet have been reluctant to realize the extent of its existence. However, we are finally becoming educated to the fact that we are all in the AIDS matter together. Because of AIDS we are being forced to learn lessons of tolerance, understanding, and acceptance.

This condition also brings out elements of people's personality and character they did not realize as part of themselves. So many of the infected individuals question, among other things, their spirituality, their unique universal existence, their fear of the unknown, and most importantly, the element of love. Our souls grow the most under the greatest stress. This is true not only for those afflicted but their families and friends as well.

During sessions with spirits who have passed with this condition, many gave reasons for having to go through this experience. The spirits prefaced their communication by explaining that their life paths were chosen long before they came to earth. Many have said that they are helping to balance the negative karma of this planet created by our wrong way of thinking about and behaving toward each other. People who have passed from cancer have told me the same thing.

I dedicate this chapter to all of those afflicted with this devastating illness; all those who have shared in helping those afflicted; and all those who have lost precious loved ones in this agonizing way.

Mommy's Little Girl

It is important to point out that the communication skills of the spirit are important, and they determine to a large degree the success of the sitting. The following session was quite impressive for two reasons. First, the child was clear, precise, and understood the process of communication. Second, whenever children come through, they are pure and speak with innocence.

One day a very distraught lady by the name of Miriam called and begged my help. She told me her little girl got AIDS and died after receiving a blood transfusion. "I can't go on living until I am sure my baby is all right," she said. I was able to give her an appointment in place of a last-minute cancellation.

When Miriam Johnson arrived, she informed me that she wasn't familiar with the work I did. She said she was at the end of her rope, and anyone who could shed even a little light would be helpful. I sat her down and explained in detail how I worked and what to expect. She was a bit nervous, but after she realized I wasn't a threat or a fake, she was able to relax and allow the experience to unfold.

I started with my usual prayer and began the reading. It took several minutes until I began to hear some slight whisperings of thought in my head.

"I do believe your young girl is here. She has long chestnut hair, bright green eyes, and an adorable smile. She seems a bit shy."

A teary-eyed Miriam responded, "Is it her? Is it really her?"

"She says yes."

"How do I know? I mean what can she tell me?"

I continued. "I am given the name of Bethie."

Miriam starts crying uncontrollably. "Yes, that was her nickname. I always called her Bethie. Her real name is Elizabeth."

"Very strange . . . she is holding something which I can't quite make out. Hold on. Oh, did she have some stuffed animals?"

"Yes, in her room."

"She mentions your giving her a stuffed animal. Wait! She is showing it to me. Hmmm, it looks like a red pony. Does that make any sense?"

"No, I don't remember her having a stuffed red pony. I guess she could have, but I don't remember."

I then telepathically asked Bethie to tell me more about the animal. After a few minutes, I continued.

"Bethie is showing me a hospital room, and you are standing there with a stuffed red pony."

A light went off in Miriam's head.

"Oh, yes, of course. John and I bought one for her, and she

held it the entire time she was in the hospital. I'm sorry I couldn't remember."

"I must say, your girl is very bright and definitely came to this earth with a mission. I love her energy and her zest for life. You would have never suspected her to die so young."

Miriam nodded her head yes, and wiped the tears from her eyes.

"She is talking about a camp. Do you remember her going to a camp?"

"Yes, it was this past summer."

"It sounds like reindeer?"

"No, it was Camp Rainier."

"That's close enough. Your daughter is showing me a medal; it has some kind of ribbon on it. Do you understand this?"

"Yes," Miriam gasped. "She won a medal. I was just looking at it. It was for rowing. She was the rowing champion."

I responded, "Yes, she was with you in the bedroom this morning when you took it out of the box."

Miriam could hardly believe what she was hearing.

"She wants to give love to John and to tell you she is okay with your decision. I'm sorry, but I have no idea what she means."

Miriam's tears started to well up in her eyes once more. She stared at me and said, "I just told John I would marry him, but I wasn't sure my little girl would like it."

"She says yes, and that she saw John bend down and give her a kiss on her forehead when she died in the hospital."

After several other incredible evidential facts, I asked Miriam if she had any questions.

"Yes. Will my little girl be in heaven when I get there?"

At that moment I was touched by such beautiful and loving emotion from little Bethie. She told me to tell her mother that not only would she be there for her but she would come to get her and bring her to heaven with her.

The session ended, and Miriam was smiling from ear to ear. She couldn't help hugging me and telling me how grateful she was. She felt that she could finally start her life over again because she knew her little girl was safe and very much alive. Once a woman of despair, Miriam had become a woman of joy.

The Heart

The beauty of my work is not only that I have enlightened others about the truth of life after death but I have witnessed incredible and miraculous changes in people because of it. The following session was one of the most touching experiences of eternal love I had ever encountered.

Many times I am given information that does not make sense to the person until later. Such was the case during my reading with a young man named Tom. As I began to tune into his energy, I noticed a young man standing at his right side. He began to describe the conditions of his death, about which I knew nothing prior to the sitting.

"I have a gentleman here who gives you a lot of love. He is standing to your right side. He has blue eyes, brown hair, and wears a beard. He died rather young. It seems he should have died later in life. Hmmm . . . Would you know who this might be?"

"Yes, I think so," Tom replied.

"He gives me a sense of being out of it as if he was on drugs. I feel he was on pain medication, something like morphine."

"Yeah, that's right."

"I also feel he had trouble breathing. I think he had to be given oxygen. I also feel very weak. It feels like a condition of AIDS. Do you understand this?"

Tom begins to cry, "Yes, I understand. That's how he died."

"He gives you his love and says he is around you all the time. He has been trying to tell you he is with you, but you don't see him, and he gets very frustrated. He says you received a promotion at work."

"Well, yeah, my supervisor just spoke to me today about the possibility."

"Your friend is laughing. He says he helped get it for you, and now you owe him."

Tom laughed.

"Do you know the name of Gary?"

"That's his name!"

"He mentions something about the front yard and your wanting to plant flowers. He shows himself watering the lawn and says something about you're not using the right flowers. Do you know what this means?"

"Yes, I think so. I went to the nursery last week and bought some flowers for the front yard. I brought them home and haven't planted them yet."

I asked, "Why not?"

"When I got home, I put them next to the others and the colors didn't match, so I have to take them back. Gary was very particular about his garden and used to water it every day. I knew he wouldn't like those colors mixed together. I don't dare plant flowers that don't fit into his color scheme. He just wouldn't like it!"

"And he doesn't," I exclaimed.

We both laughed.

"He is telling me you were in the garage looking through some boxes. He shows me photo albums. Does this make sense?"

"Yes, I was doing that this week. I'm thinking of moving, and I wanted to see what stuff to keep and what not to."

"Gary says you have already spoken to someone about selling the house, and you've been looking at one behind where you live now."

"I don't understand that."

"Gary said to wait, you will. He shows me something to do with two hearts joined together. Do you have something like this in the bedroom?"

Tom could not place the hearts. He mentally went through the house and could not picture what I was describing. I told him that it might make sense later.

"Gary wants me to tell you he loves you very much, and he always will. He wants you to know he is always with you."

Tom expressed his love back to Gary and his happiness in knowing Gary was around him.

"Gary will send you some kind of sign so you will know he is with you."

"That would be great. I can't wait."

With that, the session ended. Tom assured me that he felt a relief from the session. He recognized Gary's personality coming through in many things that were said. He thanked me and went on his way.

Four months later, Tom returned to see me, and he relayed an amazing event. He said that after his reading with me, he went home and put his tape away, not thinking any more of the session. Three weeks later, he got the promotion Gary said he would get. Tom explained further. "My coworker gave me two cards. The first was a congratulatory card for the promotion. Then she said, 'The strangest thing happened.' As she was leaving the card store, she stopped in front of another card and felt compelled to buy it. She didn't understand why, but she knew she had to give it to me. When I opened the card, it had two hearts joined together. Printed inside was the message: I LOVE YOU."

Tom said that there was something familiar about the card, so he returned home and went through all of the boxes filled with letters and cards Gary had given him. When he opened them, he understood the meaning of the card. All had been signed the exact same way: I LOVE YOU . . . *Gary.*

Mom and Dad, It's Me!

Many people who sit with me are extremely skeptical. Usually, their belief system does not allow them to open up to the possibilities of a life after death. My work challenges most conventional beliefs that are based upon years of rigid ideas and closed-minded thinking.

Around every living creature there exists an energy force referred to as the *aura*. When a spirit comes to visit you, it sees you as an energy form. Not only does it see the physical body (face, chest, legs, and so on), but it sees you on many other levels as well. In the aura, the spirit is able to see your emotional, mental, and spiritual bodies and the conditions of each one. All your thoughts, words, deeds, feelings, and health issues are contained in your auric field. Therefore, spirit beings are able to convey any illness or disease, or emotional upset you are experiencing. This information is given especially if the spirits feel that something can be done to help the individual. A spirit being is also able to re-lay any other information recorded in the aura, such as future events about which you have been thinking.

The following reading totally changed my clients' way of think-ing. Again, I reiterate that I am not responsible for who or what comes through. Someone they had not expected came through with what I thought was extraordinary information. The couple, Vivian and Paul Strauss, sat in front of me. I could tell they were skeptical, so I began immediately.

"Now, of course I don't know who you want to contact, but I must ask you, did you lose a girl?"

The couple looked inquisitively at each other and then back to me. Vivian spoke up.

"No, but what do you get with that?"

"There is a girl, a young girl about twenty, who stands with you. I'm sorry, I can't get her name. Let's just see. Maybe she will let me know who she is."

A few minutes passed.

"Vivian, there is an older lady here who belongs to your mother and speaks about Chicago?"

"Yes, that's my grandmother, my mother's mother. She lived in Chicago. What is she saying?"

"She is concerned about your mother. Does your mother have eye trouble, or has she just made an appointment with an eye doctor?"

Paul began to move uneasily in his chair. The information hit a nerve in him, and he spoke up.

"That's exactly right."

"This lady mentions that you have had trouble with your mother—that you're not speaking to her. Let me put it this way. Your mother can be a bit overwhelming, and the two of you gen-erally knock heads together. Does that make sense?"

They could not believe what I was saying. I had expressed the situation exactly as it stood.

"Yes, I don't get along with her as well as I would like," said Vivian. "She's a hard person to talk to."

"Your grandmother, her mother, wants you to treat her better. She says to have more understanding of her."

The couple nodded their heads in agreement, and I continued.

"This lady sends you a lot of love. Who is Paul?"

"That's my name," said Paul.

"There is another person in the spirit world with the same name."

Vivian and Paul looked at each other. I could see the tears well up in their eyes.

"I am told this is your son. Is that correct?"

"Yes, it is."

"Paul, I want to tell you what your boy is telling me. You need to take better care of yourself. He is very concerned about your health. He says that you have not dealt with his death, and you are holding on to the grief and not letting it out. That is harmful to your health. You need to get out and do other things. Do you like to plant?"

"Yes."

"Your son wants you to plant some flowers in the front yard."

"I was just thinking of that the other day."

"He put the thought into your head."

The couple stared at me with a blank expression. They were obviously moved by the accuracy of the information and hung on to my every word.

"This might sound very weird to you," I said, "but I must tell you that your son wants you to know he has a girlfriend over there."

Vivian placed her hands over her face and began to cry.

She murmured, "That's right. Is she okay?"

I did not understand the situation, so I asked the parents to clarify this message.

"Did his earthly girlfriend pass over as well?"

"Yes, several months after our son. She was like a daughter to us," explained Vivian.

"Oh, my God. That's incredible," I responded. "She wants you to know they are together. Oh, this is the girl who came in earlier in the session."

They both nodded their heads yes. The reading continued for a little while longer, and I relayed personality traits and the death condition of their son.

"You know, your son seems a bit wild. It was hard for him to settle down. I know he has this girl with him, but he certainly played around a lot."

"Yes, that's true. He had many girls, or at least he said that."

"I think he liked music. Do you know about the guitar in the garage?

Paul responded. "Yes, we were just looking at it. Paul wanted to play in a band. He used to practice all the time."

"He said to look at it when you go home. You will see that the second string is broken."

Paul wasn't sure but said he would check.

"He is telling me something about a car. Do you have a pickup truck?"

"Yes."

"He is telling me about new tires, or getting new tires, or needing new tires?"

I thought this man was going to have a heart attack. His face turned stone white.

"I just got them put on last Friday."

"Your boy said to check the headlight because it needs to be changed."

"Oh, my God, I just noticed that last night."

The couple were dumbfounded.

"Your son died rather quickly. I feel very strange in my head, like I am drugged, although I don't feel he died from an overdose. Rather, it has to do with the inside of his body. He keeps saying he didn't have to suffer very long, and he is happy about that. Was there something wrong with his blood?"

"Yes!"

"Did he have AIDS?"

They started to cry once again.

"Yes."

"Strange. Most people who come through with AIDS have had the condition for quite a while before their passing. I don't get that with your son. I mean, he seems to get sick and die very quickly."

"Yes. He found out he had it, and a week later he went into the hospital and died. It was very quick," the father replied.

"Did this young lady also pass with AIDS?" I asked.

"Yes," said the mother.

"She really wants to give you her love and say hello to Carrie? Do you understand? She wants to give love and a thank-you to this person."

"Carrie is her mother."

"Your boy wants to tell you he is sorry you had to go through this and that he is all right now. He is going to play music."

Vivian and Paul reached out and held each other's hands. The wish they had been praying for—a look into a brand-new world—had been fulfilled. They knew they could never have their son back, but, through me, they had much proof that he was alive on the other side. They were ready to start the process of healing. Since then, Vivian's relationship with her mother has much improved, and Paul has begun his own beautiful flower garden where he sits, meditates, and contemplates life from a new perspective.

Bye, Baby

As I mentioned before, I never know which part of a reading will have the strongest impact on a client. Much of the information seems mundane, but, of course, I realize it is provided for proof. There are times when I will receive a message in my head and rationalize the thought because I think I am influencing the information, or it is too inconsequential. However, I find out later that the particular word, phrase, or description was especially meaningful to a client. No matter how many years I have been involved in this work, I find that I am constantly learning to trust my communication with spirit. The following session is a wonderful example of how something so trivial can change a person's life forever.

I attended a group meeting at a woman's house in San Bernardino, California. After I read for three of the people present, I turned to a young lady sitting by herself on the couch. Her name was Laurie. I relayed a half-hour message from her grandmother, who described the family possessions and who owned certain items of hers, and where they were placed around the house.

I was close to the end when the spirit of a young man emerged and sat right next to the girl. He seemed to hold her hand in his. He started to send me information.

"I must tell you that I see a man sitting next to you. He says he is the reason you are here tonight. Do you understand this?"

I thought Laurie was going to faint. Her face turned white, and her eyes bulged as she tried to restrain her tears.

Her lips separated, and she said, "Yes, is he here?"

"I have a man who says he loves you, and he is very sorry. He is sorry about what he did."

Laurie wiped her tears and looked at me with a jubilant smile.

"He is giving me an initial *M* for a name. I see. It is an *M* at the beginning and a *Y* at the end?"

"Yes, that's it. His name is Marty."

"Was he your boyfriend?"

"Yes."

"He speaks about some trouble, and that he wasn't honest with you about things."

"I know. It's all right. Please tell him it's all right."

I then explained to Laurie how she could send him thoughts on her own and didn't need me to communicate them.

"Marty feels like a tough guy to me. He has a very good sense of humor, but I must say he seems a bit twisted with it. Do you understand that? I mean, he says things that are totally off the wall, and people might get the wrong idea of what he is trying to say."

Laurie grinned with understanding. She said he would often "freak people out" with what he would say.

"He says something about how you were supposed to live together, but you couldn't, or there was some trouble with that. He is telling me too many people tried to interfere. Do you understand?"

"Well, my mom didn't really like Marty and didn't want us together, so she gave us a lot of hassle when we talked about moving in together."

"He understands. He tells me he had a checkered past, and you helped to straighten him out. I think he was hanging out with the wrong people."

Laurie nodded in agreement.

I continued. "I do believe he was heavily into drugs. I think this is where he caught the virus—sharing needles. Do you know anything about this?"

"I don't know. He wouldn't tell me. I assumed that is how he got it. He was pretty bad before I met him."

"He tells me you were the best thing that ever happened to him. It is a bit ironic. He is talking about an engagement. Were you planning to get married?"

Laurie begins to weep once again.

"We were talking about it. He said he wanted to, and we were talking about setting a date."

"He is telling me about an engagement ring. He said he picked it out for you."

Laurie broke down. After several minutes, she showed us a diamond engagement ring that she wore on a chain around her neck.

Through her tears, she explained. "His mother found this with a letter that had my name on it. He was planning to give it to me the day of his death."

Everyone in the room gasped at the same time. I waited a few minutes until Marty supplied more information.

"He wants to thank you for taking care of him. Did you help to feed and bathe him?"

"Yes, I took care of him. No one else really wanted any part of him. I didn't mind; I loved him."

"That was very kind of you. You were being tested by spirit, and you certainly passed the test."

During the rest of the reading, Marty continued to thank Laurie for straightening out his life and for helping him while he was sick. He tried to convey that he still loved her. Laurie believed she was talking to the spirit of her deceased lover, but I could tell she had some reservations. My energy was decreasing, and I was instructed by my guides to stop for the evening.

I thanked everyone and turned to Laurie and said, "Marty says, bye, baby."

Laurie stood up and let out a shriek. I asked her if she was all right and she exclaimed: "Last night when I thought of Marty, I said to him: If this guy is real, and you do come through, call me by my nickname. My nickname is *Baby*."

With that, we all uttered a collective gasp and rolled our heads in amazement at spirit and the power of love.

CHAPTER 7

Suicide

As living individuals, we are made up of everything we have ever experienced in past lifetimes. In other words, our present lifetime is a compilation of past thoughts, actions, and deeds, positive or negative, that we have brought with us. Because of past karma, we find ourselves being reborn into certain family situations with a particular economic and social status that is necessary for our spiritual growth.

Before coming into an earthly incarnation, a soul prepares for its new life in the spiritual realms. It is common for a soul to return to a field of work in which it had previous lifetimes of interest or experience. Let's say a soul plans to experience earth life in the year 2021 as a medical professional. It will spend time with its guides and teachers perfecting necessary skills and will look into medical breakthroughs and technologies that will be available at that time. It may also become aware of new diseases or scourges that will affect humankind, and it will learn how to help spread knowledge and love to everyone through its potential work on earth. As a soul becomes aware of this knowledge, it is integrated into a new personality. It is vital the soul understands the value of its participation in the future of humankind and how it will affect the lives of many others.

As spiritual beings, we are forever learning, developing, and evolving. We look at our future incarnation as sort of a blueprint of what we are attempting to accomplish and learn as we walk in the physical body. Therefore, we pick opportunities and experiences on the earth that are optimum for our spiritual growth and awareness. Our karma is intertwined with the timing of our next incarnation and our experience in it.

Ultimately, we all are here to learn *love*. It may sound simple, but by and large, it is not easy. Love has many aspects. One of the first lessons we are attempting to learn is a love of self. Without love and awareness of self, we will not know how to love others. Once we have mastered such unconditional love of self and others, we become enlightened and have respect for the natural law of cause and effect—not because we want a better position in life but rather because we know it is the only way. By understanding this law, and by living it, we come to respect each other's uniqueness. Then we can live in accordance with our fellow human beings for the betterment of all.

The Inclination Toward Suicide

This earth is a place to experience elements and aspects of the human condition we cannot experience anywhere else. It is a place of growth, and growth is never easy. Most people alive today are constantly challenged with worries of survival. We are bombarded by financial, employment, emotional, or health concerns. Many times these worries are associated with feelings of self-destruction. We think, *I can't get through this,* or *I would be better off dead*.

It is quite common for most people to feel suicidal at least once in their lives. However, this feeling comes and goes as situations change. The type of personality who is obsessed with the

idea of self-destruction and makes several attempts to end his or
her life usually belongs to one of the following categories:

1. A person with a controlling personality, and who feels out
   of control with his situation.
2. A person who has a very negative self-image. She sees herself as worthless because she feels she contributes nothing
   to society. She thinks that the planet would be a better
   place without her.
3. Those who are terminally ill and don't want to go through
   the pain and suffering of dying.
4. Those who are mentally ill or have a biochemical imbalance.

It is understandable that because of certain feelings, circumstances, and beliefs, one could find a perfect rationale for doing
away with one's life. However, from a spiritual point of view, it is not
right. We each have a destiny to which we are born. Our karmic destiny may last for only one month, or thirty-five years, or eighty years.
Before we return to this earth, we fill ourselves with a strong desire
for birth and physical experience, and we enter this world with a
timing mechanism built into our psychic web. When life is cut short,
our physical body ceases to exist, but we must understand that the
magnetic ties we have to the earth are still active. These ties are sev-
ered only when we have completed our preordained time on the
physical plane. For as it is written, *Every season has its time.*

When a person kills himself, one of the first things he realizes
is that he is not dead. He has an overwhelming feeling of being
very heavy because the earth ties are still part of his nature. In a
way, we can say the soul is not totally free. The mortal personality
dies, but not the immortal soul. The soul remains stuck between
the physical world and the spiritual world—alive but unable to
communicate with loved ones or anyone else. The soul feels guilt,
pain, and anguish for a life cut short. He learns of his destiny and
how beneficial and meaningful his life would have been if he had
stayed alive. In the spiritual state, he becomes aware of why he

had to go through the particular experiences that drove him to suicide. He also senses the grief and anger of those he left behind. The most unfortunate circumstance is that he finds himself in a limbo state. He is not able to go to the heaven worlds, nor is he able to return to the physical world. He is stuck in "no-man's-land" with the constant memory of his horrific act. He sees his death over and over again, and it plays like a bad movie. He is trapped, and there is no way out of the theater.

While some are conscious of what they have done, many suicide victims may not even be aware that they have passed over. On the whole, these souls automatically relive their final death over and over again. The suicide act becomes an endless loop, and it can be pretty gruesome. Eventually, the time comes when they realize that they are actually dead to the physical plane.

The Spiritual View of Suicide

Behind any act there is a powerful force known as motive. It is this motive that is the determining factor, not only for a suicide but for every action in our lives. Through motive comes action, and we create actions based on motives. As I have stated many times, there is a natural law of cause and effect. In other words, action is a direct result of motive.

In the case of terminally ill or elderly persons, some are sick and want to save their families time, money, and heartache by committing suicide. These persons are unaware of the spiritual side of their actions. Perhaps before coming into the physical plane, family members set up certain conditions and situations in order to work out their group karma. Or they needed to experience being of service to the one who is ill. Furthermore, some argue that assisted suicide is best—it stops suffering and gives death some dignity. But who can play God? How do we know that a soul didn't choose to go through an experience of a fatal illness in order to burn away karma? If we cut short someone's natural time on earth, we never know whether something valuable could have been learned or whether such an experience was necessary to reach a new spiritual plateau.

In any event, when suicide occurs, a soul will have to go through and learn the experience again, having to return in another lifetime with the same or similar ailment. The ailment may not be as extreme as it was in a previous life because part of it has already been lived out. Usually, a soul has to exhaust a disease so it can never be affected by it again.

There are two exceptions to the wrongdoing of suicide:

1. If suicide is brought about by individuals who are mentally ill or have a biochemical imbalance. In such situations, these persons are not completely conscious of their decisions. When they pass over, they find themselves in sort of a "ward" where they are helped to heal their mental conditions and their soul nature is restored to its proper state.

2. The second exception to suicide is a soul who comes back to the physical world before its proper time and is not mature enough to handle the lessons it thought it could. Even though a soul thinks it has certain strength, it arrives on earth and does not feel comfortable. Those with this shortcoming have often said prior to their death words to the effect: *I don't fit in,* or *I don't think it's the right time for me.*

Because it is the nature of a soul to grow and learn, we always bring into our lives specific situations to overcome or balance out. If we realize that while on earth it is normal to experience physical, mental, or emotional pain, and suicide *does not* take away any of it, I believe there would be fewer suicides. We need to educate ourselves, and especially our young people, about the "wrongs" of suicide and accentuate the responsibility of living life fully.

How Can the Living Help the Dead?

Many people have asked me: *What should be done with the body of one who has committed suicide?* The body is just a shell. Upon leaving the shell, the spirit feels no attachment to it whatsoever. It is like a worn-out piece of clothing. In the case of suicide or a tragic accident, it is important that the body be cremated. If a spirit is somewhat in an earthbound state, cremation destroys the body quickly, and the spirit will no longer feel any physical ties to it. It will be easier for the soul to become aware of its new situation.

We must realize that this problem has no simple solution because the circumstances surrounding each suicide are different. But we can help those who have committed this terrible mistake. It is important to understand that our thoughts are the only way to get through to such victims. First, we can send thoughts to individuals and tell them to stop wasting their energy by trying to get back into the physical world. They must realize that they have passed out of the physical body. Next, we can then send them thoughts of love, peace, and forgiveness. By sending these beautiful thoughts, tormented souls will be comforted, and they will become more aware of their situation.

As I stated above, there are many different reasons behind an act of self-destruction, but the result is the same for all. To this day, I have not had one spirit come through and tell me it is happy with its decision, nor would it commit such an act again. Quite the contrary. All suicide victims share a sense of regret for the crime against their soul. I can say all of those who have come back have warned others not to repeat their mistakes. The suicide act slowed their spiritual progress, and they had a very difficult time forgiving themselves.

I have chosen the following sessions as examples of circumstances and reasons why people commit suicide, and their reactions when they are finally able to talk to loved ones. Many times I have been unable to reach a suicide victim simply because he or she was unaware or in a limbo state.

I'm Sorry!

The following case clearly demonstrated a disturbed spirit who, after destroying her life, wanted nothing more than to prove to her loved ones that she was with them and was in need of forgiveness. It also showed the confusion of those left behind. Halfway through the reading, the sitter broke down and begged the spirit for forgiveness because she felt responsible for her friend's act of suicide.

I was about to perform a monthly demonstration in the Hollywood United Methodist Church. My living room, which was the usual place for my demonstrations, had grown too small to accommodate the crowd that was in attendance that night. My living room held thirty people, the church held two hundred.

The sky was quite ominous that evening. I thought it would open up at any moment and flood the streets with pouring rain. I stood right at the altar looking toward the enormous crowd. The moment seemed so strange. I looked at the crowd, and then looked at my surroundings. I could not believe I was doing a séance in a church. I laughed to myself and thought, *Ha, if my family priest could see me now!* I began my meditation, and as I recited it, I heard the sound of raindrops hitting the roof. It was no simple rain shower. It was a downpour! A clamorous sound of thunder was heard, and a brilliant blaze of lightning followed closely behind. The lightning lit up the stained-glass windows. It was quite a spectacle—Spielberg could not have done better!

I said to the congregation before me, "Well, if you weren't scared before, I bet you are now!"

As with all group meetings or demonstrations, I never know who will come through first. In this case, as in most, I began to hear the thoughts of a spiritual being.

"There is a woman here, and she keeps giving me the name of Susan."

I immediately heard a woman cry out in the second pew on my left side. I looked at her and said, "Do you understand this?"

"I'm not sure," she replied. "I mean, I know someone with that name."

I continued. "She says to me, you know her mother."

"I was just speaking to her mother yesterday. We had words."

The woman let out another shrill cry, as if she were going out of control.

Everyone looked over to her. It was obvious that she was in some terrible pain. I waited for a few moments.

"This woman wants to come to you. It is strange, but she does not feel like family to you. Yet, she is quite close to you and says she loves you."

The woman bowed her head. I went on.

"She gives me the name of Kathy. Do you understand this?"

The woman wiped the tears from her eyes, and without looking up, the words trickled out of her mouth. "That's her name."

"She is telling me you just started a new job, and she wants you to know she helped you get it. She also shows me two kitty cats, one with gray stripes, and the other white with black spots. She is referring to them as your kids."

"Yes, those are my cats, that's right. Does she see them in the house?" she asked.

"Yes, she wants you to know she does. She talks about the bell they play with in the kitchen. I think this is tied to a doorknob."

The woman nodded.

"She is showing me a house. Now this house seems different. Hmmm . . . It is a wooden house. I would say blond wood. It looks like a mountain house. It has a wooden railing going around the outside porch. Do you know this house?"

"Yes, it was ours."

"She tells me you had plans of rebuilding something or adding on something. This is funny, she keeps referring to the contractors as jerks."

The woman spoke up. "Yeah, we were redoing an outside wall near the porch and we couldn't get the right contractor. We kept getting screwed around by them."

"She is showing me a picture. The picture is in a heart-shaped frame. Do you understand this?"

"Yes, it is the picture I have of Kathy. It is the only one I have of her. Please tell her that I am sorry."

"She knows you are sorry, but says it wasn't your fault. Do you understand this?"

"No, it was my fault. It's because of me she's dead."

I listened quite clearly and suddenly felt a gun in my mouth.

"I feel a gun in my mouth. The barrel feels quite cool. I'm sorry, but I feel as though she killed herself with a gun in her mouth. Is that correct?"

The woman gasped and answered, "Yes."

"You know, I feel that before she died she was screaming and yelling. Was there a big fight that she was in?"

"Yes."

"She said she was very confused and locked herself in the bedroom for a couple of hours."

"Yes. We fought. That's right. Please tell her I'm so sorry, and I love her very much."

"Yes, she knows this," I replied.

"Your friend is telling me that it was her decision to kill herself. At the time she wanted you to feel guilty and knows now this was not right and asks your forgiveness for the pain she has caused you. She wants you to know she didn't have the courage to end the relationship with you, and the thought of someone else was too hard for her to deal with. Does this make sense to you?"

"Yes, that's it. I understand, but I will never forgive myself."

"You have to. You didn't pull the trigger. You tried to talk with her, but she wouldn't listen. You can't play God. Understand your friend couldn't find the love within herself to realize that she was special. She came back to tell you it was not your fault."

The woman seemed to hear what I was saying. The session went on for another couple of minutes until I went on to another message for someone else in the congregation.

During the break, the woman came up to me and hugged me. She said, "I never believed in this before, but I knew it was Kathy who came through." The message from Kathy had helped her tremendously. She said, "There was just too much proof that it was her." She continued to say how she would try and work on forgiving herself and would pray to Kathy and ask for her help.

Later I learned that this woman had been having an affair with another woman. When she told Kathy that she did not want to continue their relationship and it was time to move on, they argued for some time. Kathy went into the bedroom, got a gun, and loaded it. Then she locked herself in the bathroom, stuck the gun in her mouth, and shot herself.

One last thing. Kathy had mentioned to her friend that the memory of her death still haunted her but that she was getting help from people in spirit.

It's Never Too Late to Say I Love You

It is truly a shame when a young man who has everything to live for decides to take his own life. The family immediately feels guilty and thinks that they could have prevented it in some way. The spirit of the man is not only ashamed but finds it difficult to forgive and love himself once again.

The following was just such a case. A young man returned to talk to his mother about the love he never realized until it was too late. Although there was an enormous amount of pain and heartache present, there was also optimism. It was one of the most moving readings, and the closest I had ever come to experiencing the true meaning of unconditional love. When love is so strong, there is no judgment.

When I answered the door, there stood a medium-sized woman with a beautiful smile and soft skin. She seemed to be in her late fifties, and she radiated a sense of peace and self-assurance. She was quite well-spoken and was down to earth about herself and life in general.

At the start, she stated that she had never been to a séance and didn't give what I did a lot of credence, but her therapist felt it might help her to resolve issues from her past. She said that to live in the now, she was "game to try anything." "Besides," she continued, "I like to look at all of my options." With those words, I felt an immediate kinship with this woman. She had a wonderfully charming personality and a splendid and refreshing sense of humor. She reminded me of "Aunt Bea" from *The Andy Griffith Show*. Of course, I had no facts or information regarding her or the person she wanted to reach. I asked, "Are you comfortable?" She responded, "I feel beautiful." With that, I began the reading.

"There is a man standing behind you, and he tells me to say happy birthday to you."

"Well, thank you very much. My birthday was two days ago."

I continued. "This man is very close to you, and he mentions something about going to Africa or being in Africa. Does this make sense to you?"

"Yes, it does. My husband and I spend a great deal of time there, and we hope to go back soon. Isn't that something?"

"Do you have a son and a daughter?"

"No, just two boys."

"This man behind me is telling me something about a son. I am not sure if he is your son, or talking about your son."

"I don't know."

"Hold on. Huh, I see. Your youngest son passed. Is that correct?"

"Yes, that is."

"He is here. He is the one behind you. He is very perplexed because he can't believe we are doing this. Or, that you are doing this."

"That makes terrible sense."

"Do you understand about a collection of old tribal artifacts?"

"Yes, my husband deals in antiques. Our house is just full of them. My goodness, this is quite amazing."

"I am given the name of Andrew or Andy?"

"That is his name. We called him Andy. He was named after his father."

"He shows me a beautiful house and on the walls are beautiful oil paintings. They seem to be from all over the world. It looks very much like a museum."

"That is correct. My, you are amazing! I collect art, mostly oils, and have a rather extensive collection. My goodness."

I could tell the woman was trying to figure out just how I was getting this information.

"He is also showing me some sort of exotic material. Blankets or throws. You have them throughout the house as well. In fact, he shows them hanging on the walls."

She shook her head.

"What is this about living in the back? Andy talks about living in the back."

"We have a guest house, and Andy used it as an art studio. He spent most of his time there."

I concurred. "That is why he is showing me such beautiful colors. Yes, I actually see an artist's palette."

The meeting continued for at least another half-hour with some incredible evidence of life after death. Andy described in some detail where he was and what he was experiencing.

"He is telling me that when he first got there, he was at a hospital of some sort. He said they helped him with his mental condition. He tells me that now he is living in an artists' colony where everyone is involved with their own particular artful expression. He is saying that he is meeting people whom he understands and who understand him. He is learning a lot more about everything these days."

He then proceeded to talk about his relationship with his mother, and how he died.

"Your son was a very sensitive person. I feel that he was quite unhappy. Not really unhappy, but rather depressed. I feel he could not keep his emotions under control. Did he take drugs of some sort?"

"Yes. Andy was on medication prescribed by his doctor for a manic-depressive condition. He was also a user of illegal drugs as well."

"Hmmm. Yes, I know he was on drugs of some sort, but I have to tell you that he definitely thinks there was a chemical imbalance, and it led to his death. He is telling me that he often told you he hated you."

"Yes, he did."

"You know of course he didn't mean it. He was sick."

"Oh yes, I am aware of that."

"He wants you to know it was the drugs and his own frustration talking. He didn't see it from your point of view until he passed. He said you tried helping him for years and would never give up. He is saying that you never even raised your voice to him when he had done something wrong."

The woman moved uncomfortably in her chair, then spoke. "I don't know about that. But, yes, I loved my son. I realized he had a problem. What else is a mother supposed to do? I loved him no matter what and supported him."

I jumped in. "Even through the rough times. From what he says, he treated you terribly, and you just took it."

"I understood what was going on. At least I tried the best I could to understand. I did what I could for Andy to make sure he was safe. I wanted him to be happy, but he was always a loner. I loved him and always will. His father and I tried our best, although I think his father lost patience. But in a strange way, I understood Andy. I felt as though at times I could see right through to his soul. I knew how miserable he was. I felt terrible that he suffered so."

"He is sorry about what he put you through."

"He has no need to be. I love him."

The reading then shifted and was very emotionally charged as Andy described his own death.

"Your son is in the back of the house feeling very distraught. He is having thoughts of ending it all. He feels as though he can't go on. He keeps looking around at his paintings. He wonders what is going to happen to them when he dies. Then he just doesn't seem to care anymore. He feels so depressed. There is so much hatred of self here. He feels unstable. Were you away at the time of his death?"

"Yes, we were. Actually, we got back from our trip that afternoon. His father found him."

"Your son is showing me a field behind the house. It looks like a field or a long backyard."

"That is correct. This is quite incredible. I just don't know what to say, but that it is absolutely correct."

I interrupted the reading to ask her if she was okay and if she wanted to continue. She said she was and that I was to continue by all means.

"Your son shows me a big tree. It looks like an oak. Very big and thick. He climbs up."

Immediately, I began to feel my throat tighten, and I couldn't breathe. I instantly felt the death condition because Andrew conveyed exactly what he went through. At this point I stopped the reading and asked Andrew to please show me the death visually so that I did not have to feel it. I also asked my guides to please watch over this communication since the spirit was not able to control his death situation. After several minutes, I continued with the reading. Andrew visually impressed me with the scene of his death.

"Your son hanged himself from an oak tree in the backyard. He climbed up a ladder to one of its branches. Does that sound right to you?"

Andrew's mother began to weep. She took a tissue out of her bag, wiped her eyes, and acknowledged the information as correct.

I continued. "I feel so bad. This is so amazing. I have rarely felt or have seen something this way. Your boy left his body from his head."

Andy shows himself floating above his body.

"He can't believe he is dead because he feels so alive. He thinks he screwed something up and is trying very hard to get back into his body through his head. He can't do it, and he is getting very frustrated. He begins to cry!"

I was overcome by this experience. I kept telling the mother about the amazing vision I was seeing. After a few moments, I continued once again.

"Andy says he waited around not sure of what to do. He saw his dad find him, and he was so upset. Andy realized immediately that what he did was wrong. He felt badly for you and his father. He watched his father tell you and saw you break down. He heard your thoughts about how you always knew this was going to happen. He also felt your feelings of love. He felt quite horrible about the way he made you feel."

"Please tell him I understand."

"He says, thank you, Mom. Forgive me. I love you very much, and I love my dad too. I'm getting help here, Mom. They have some nice people who have seen to it that I get back to myself again. It was too hard, Mom."

I explained to the woman that the spirit has free will, and it may come back into an incarnation at the wrong time. "When this happens, a person will usually go through his life feeling a tremendous amount of *not fitting in*." I continued to say that her son didn't fit in because it was not the proper time for his soul to experience earth life. His soul had not matured enough to go through what had been placed before it. "Very often, it is too overwhelming and the soul looks for escape. That is why a person commits suicide."

The woman totally understood what I was saying. She informed me that Andy never fit in. She said, "Even as a small child, he seemed very different from his other brother and most of the children his age." In a way, this reading confirmed the concept of returning to earth too soon.

The mother was so very pleased she had made contact with her son. She said that she hoped for a miracle one day, and that day had come. She told Andy that she would live the rest of her life with him in mind so he could experience a little bit of earth through her.

I bid a good-bye to this woman and felt blessed that day for being in the presence of a wise, old soul. She knew the meaning of seeing love in everyone and in every experience.

My Mother and Father

One of the most devastating experiences a family faces is when another family member takes her own life. Not only is there an empty void that cannot be filled, but a never-ending onslaught of questions haunt them. *Why did she do this? Could I have stopped her? Is she sorry for what she did? What will happen to her next?*

In any given year, thousands of individuals go through the devastating experience of a family member committing suicide. Although I am only one individual and am limited to the number of people I see, I receive much satisfaction when I am able to answer questions through their loved ones in spirit.

In the following reading, I was also able to provide much-needed insight into the motivation behind the spirit's idea of life, and why she behaved a certain way while on earth. The information was valuable for the sitter for two reasons. It not only resolved her feelings about the suicide but provided answers to questions about her relationship with her parents—a relationship she had struggled her whole life to understand. A healing took place, and her life has never been the same since.

I opened the door to a very attractive woman whose name was Nancy. She was quite charming and also a bit apprehensive and nervous. I immediately sat with her in the living room and spoke to her about what the evening would reveal. She explained to me that she was a little uncomfortable and spooked about attempting to make contact with the spirit world. I reassured her that there was nothing to fear or to be nervous about. I told her that I worked with the Christ light of love, and if for any reason she felt uncomfortable during the session, we would stop.

Nancy asked what I meant by the "Christ light of love," and I explained that it is a pure, nonjudgmental love of the highest caliber that was embodied by the master known as Jesus. This is the same love on which most Christian religions are based. I always ask for this light of love or light of protection when doing my work.

She told me that she trusted me, and we slowly ascended the stairs to the séance room. After I said my opening prayer, I began.

"Nancy, an Egyptian guide who works with me informs me that your family is present. He is telling me that the ones with whom you wish to speak are indeed here."

Nancy stared at me with her big blue eyes. Her mouth dropped open, and she was speechless.

"Standing behind you is a lady. She is wearing a greenish dress and looks quite pretty. She has light brown hair. I could describe her smile as small but sweet. I know that sounds strange. Her eyes are a beautiful blue. She says to tell you she is all right now."

Nancy continued to stare at me.

"I feel this person is a mother figure. Does the name Joan mean anything to you?"

"Yes, that's my mother's name, and she died. And how you described her is exactly what she looked like."

"I think she is much younger than you remember her. Yes, she is telling me you have a wedding photo of her, and this is what she looks like in spirit."

"Yes, I was looking at it last night."

Nancy wiped some tears from her eyes. She repeated how she couldn't believe it, how it was just incredible. I went on with the reading.

"Your mom wants you to know she has seen Margaret and Katherine."

"Margaret is her mother, and Katherine is her sister," Nancy replied.

"She also mentions the name of John. Do you know that name?"

"Oh, my God, John is my husband. That's his name. Does Mom see him?"

"Yes, she does. She wants to say hello to him and to tell him to take care of you."

Nancy was totally in awe. She shook her head in disbelief.

"Nancy, your mother gives me the feeling that she was quite ill before she passed. I feel there were a lot of drugs or pills. Does that make sense?"

"Yeah, that's right."

"Would you know about your dad finding her? I think it was on the floor in the bedroom?"

"Yeah. Dad found her."

"Your mom is feeling very sorry. She is asking for your forgiveness. She says she didn't mean to cause you such upset. I must tell you that I feel your mother was not mentally all there. Was she often depressed?"

"Uh-huh. She was. I don't know what it was, but Mom was always sick. I mean, even as a child, I remember her that way."

"Your mom is apologizing for not being a good mother to you. Was she in and out of mental institutions?"

"Yes, most of her life. She suffered from manic depression."

I quickly responded. "I knew it. She feels off center. She was someone who let life happen to her instead of making it happen. She is trying to let you know that she loves you very much and is sorry about not being able to tell you this when she was alive. I think your mother didn't understand love and wasn't sure how to give it."

"That sounds so right. My God."

"Nancy, I think your mother's mental condition was responsible for her death. Did she kill herself?"

Nancy began to cry.

"Yes. I tried to help her, but she wouldn't let me near her. I think she was just too depressed. I tried, James, but I just didn't know how to handle her. Is there something I could have done to stop her or prevent it from happening?"

"No, your mom was her own worst enemy. You could not have stopped it. Your mother would not have listened to you. Your mom didn't listen to many people."

Nancy smiled and shook her head.

"Your mom is sorry she couldn't be a mother to you. She didn't mean to hurt you. She wants me to tell you she loves the animals."

"Oh, God, yes. My mom just adored animals."

"She has Skippy or Skipper with her. What is that?"

Nancy's eyes got larger, and her mouth dropped some more.

"That was our dog when I was growing up. Mom loved him. Oh, they were such good friends. Skipper used to sleep right next to her every night. James, can I ask you, is Mom happy? I mean is she in an okay place and what will happen to her? Where will she go?"

I sent out the question mentally to her mother, Joan, and waited several minutes for a response. Sometimes when asking a spirit a question, it takes a certain amount of time to understand the question and then formulate an answer back to me.

After a few minutes I said, "Your mother wants me to tell you that she has received help from another lady. Sort of a counselor. Your mother stopped her own life but not consciously. She really was mentally out of it. Since passing, she has been working to change her mental condition and to learn how to bring her own love back into her heart. To recognize love in herself. She is in a good place, very much like earth, but more beautiful. She says that even though she is dead, she is not resting. Far from it. She is trying in her own way to make up for lost time."

From that point on, the session took on a whole new aspect. I continued to give Nancy messages from her mother.

"She wants you to know that she is fine. She is with her family but still has work to do on herself. She knows that no one can do it for her, and she has to do it herself. Your mother felt awful about your dad. She is going on about how she felt responsible. I don't understand what this means."

"I do." With that, Nancy started to cry once again.

"Okay, let me continue. Your father, hmmm. Is your father a gentle type of soul? I must tell you, as your mother speaks about your father, I immediately pick up the vibration of a man. He is standing next to me. Did your dad pass over?"

"Yes, he died a little bit after Mom. Is he all right? I need to know, please tell me. Can he hear me?"

"Yes, your dad is all right. He is with your mom. He says all he wanted was to be with your mother, and now he is. He is talking about how different it all is where they are. He pictured heaven to be a place with angels and harps, and he hasn't found any yet. He is in the country. He is going on about how stupid he was."

"Yes, go on."

"This is very strange. Did your father ever like horses?"

"Well, he grew up on a farm. I'm sure they had horses, but I'm not sure. I—"

At that moment I cut her off because her father told me something else.

"No, your dad says racehorses. He used to love racehorses. He gambled on them."

"Oh, my God, that's right. Every Saturday he went to the track. That's incredible. Is he still doing that?"

"He says he can if he wants to. They have such things there, but they don't exchange money. It is more or less done for the sportsmanship of it all. Nancy, your dad is saying to tell you he let you down. He is sorry, but he was so lonely. He let you down."

Nancy commented, "I understand, Dad. It was hard."

"Nancy, I don't know what this means. Your father is showing me a gun. It looks like a forty-five, but, forgive me, I don't know one gun from another. It's a handgun, but not small. He shows it to me. He is also showing me a room, sort of a den. There is a deck and bookshelves all around. I also see a duck decoy."

"He collected them."

"Your father shows me a pool of blood, and he is leaning back on a chair. God, did he shoot himself?"

Nancy burst into tears and mouthed the word *yes*.

I was in shock. One suicide was enough, but both parents was unthinkable. I felt such sorrow in my heart and such compassion and sympathy for Nancy. I had to take a few minutes to calm myself down. I just couldn't believe it.

"I'm sorry, Nancy, I don't mean to be graphic, but I need to give you what I get. Your dad shot himself through his left temple. He says you know this. Is that right?"

"Yes, I was the one who found him. I tried calling him all day, but he never picked up the phone, so I went to his house on the way home from work. I walked into his study and found him leaning back on his chair. His gun was lying on the floor below his arm."

"Oh, I'm so sorry. That is awful. Your dad says to tell you that he was wrong. He didn't know how to go on without your mother. He said he also didn't want to be a burden to you and John. You had your own lives. This is quite interesting. I have heard this before. Your dad is saying he didn't have to wait around too long over there because his life was close to an end anyway."

"What does he mean?"

I explained to Nancy that when someone commits suicide, he is still tied to earth until it is his natural time to die. Her father's lifespan would have been over soon. When he killed himself, the time left in the physical level was relatively short. I also conveyed to Nancy that her father was met by her mother.

Nancy then asked, "How could she?"

"Your mother was on a slightly higher level in the spiritual world. Those on a higher level can indeed return to lower levels and assist others. However, the ones on a lower level cannot go higher until they have earned it."

This idea seemed a bit perplexing to Nancy, but this was her first introduction into the metaphysical world. I reassured her that the more she studied metaphysics, the more the idea would make sense to her.

"Nancy, your dad wants me to tell you he is happy once again. He is with your mom."

"That makes me so happy. God, I was worried about him. I'm so happy he is okay, and they are together. Right?"

"Yes, they are together. Funny, your dad is mentioning a lake, or a house on a lake. He says your mom has been watching him fish from a pier. I don't know what this means."

"I do. When I was a little girl, we had a summer house on a lake, and my father used to take us fishing at the pier. He taught me how to fish."

"Well, your father wants you to know he is in heaven."

"If Dad is fishing, he is in heaven."

With that, we closed the meeting and thanked the spirit people and our guides. I also added a special prayer for Nancy to use the information for her healing. I know my prayer was answered because as she was leaving, she turned to me, still with tears in her eyes, and said, "James, I don't know what to say. That was a miracle. I feel so light. I feel such peace. It's a peace I have been searching for over ten years but was never able to find. Thank you so much in helping me to find it. It was so special. God bless you!"

Capital Punishment

I want to include in this chapter two more ideas about a premature end to life. Although neither capital punishment nor medical intervention are the same as suicide, these two issues also deal with the interruption of a soul's destiny. In saying that, I want to point out that not only is suicide wrong, but so is capital punishment.

One of the worst things imaginable is one human being taking the life of another before his or her time. It is a devastating and horrendous act, and one that seems totally unforgivable. In the case of murder, there is the added gravity that justice must be served. There is an incredible sense that by ridding society of the villain, such a brutal act will be vindicated. But that is not really true. Add to this the argument that tax money can be saved by a speedy execution, and capital punishment becomes acceptable.

Yes, it is wrong for one to take the life of another, and it is true under any circumstance, including capital punishment. I ask you to stop a moment and look at this situation from a spiritual point of view and not from an emotional standpoint. Our universe is much larger than we can conceive, and we need to start looking at this situation and every act through spiritual eyes. God, in such incredible wisdom, has created a rhythm to all life. The sun rises and sets, the planets rotate around the sun, the tides ebb and flow, and so, too, each soul has a rhythm of dawning and ending. Because of this rhythm, there is a natural time for a soul to leave this world and return once again to the world of the spirit. And only God knows the whole plan.

When a person is violently taken out of the physical body before the predetermined, natural time for the soul to leave, there are spiritual consequences. As in suicide, the magnetic tides of the soul must stay within the earthly atmosphere until its natural time to leave. When a spirit of an individual is forced out of the body by capital punishment, the personality of the criminal remains exactly the same as it was prior to execution. When it reaches the other side, it is usually scared and angry because more than likely it is not highly evolved and is ignorant of spiritual laws. In most cases, such a soul roams endlessly throughout the lower astral world with other like-minded souls. Because these tormented souls carry a mind-set of anger and hatred, they often seek revenge for their untimely deaths. They search the earth for weak-minded humans whom they can mentally influence to kill or hurt others. Sounds like a movie, doesn't it? But it is very true.

The best thing we can do is to rehabilitate and educate those in our prison system about the sanctity of life. I know it sounds like a pipe dream, but if we destroy someone before his soul's time, we take away all chances for reformation and rehabilitation. It only takes an instant for someone to see the Light of God and be transformed. Such a rehabilitated individual may one day help to prevent someone else from destroying another life. The door to growth and enlightenment must always be kept open.

By capital punishment, we continue the propagation of violence upon one another. Let's not be so quick to throw the switch without thinking about the consequences of our actions. By understanding the spiritual ramifications, we can begin to adjust our beliefs and not be so hasty to sanction a death sentence. Our society has a spiritual and ethical responsibility to assist these unevolved and tormented souls. Let's not treat them like yesterday's garbage.

Please understand that I do not condone murder. I want to point out that a person who takes the life of another does so because he has not yet fully evolved to an awareness of his own divine self. If one is in full awareness of his Godself, he would know that killing someone is not even an option. Who are we to judge one another? Do we know enough about the laws of life to play God? I assure you that we are not that powerful. Again, we must keep our minds open and learn to look at things from a spiritual and responsible perspective.

Lifesaving Machines

When someone is kept alive on lifesaving equipment such as a respirator, I believe that once again a divine plan is at work. For every disease or health crisis, there is growth, an evolution of sorts, from which we as individuals and society as a whole can learn. Medical breakthroughs and innovative technology are a part of this growth. Every discovery happens in its right time. Perhaps there would be other incredible breakthroughs and inventions if man's ego weren't ruled so much by political or financial gain.

However, mankind has been given great knowledge to create that which can be used to assist people in living more productive and quality lives. Many lives have been saved by modern medical technology, including the potent medications and vaccinations unknown a century ago. Science should be proud of these accomplishments, especially its ability to sustain the quality of a person's life. The key word is *quality*. Medical professionals are not here to play God, nor could they even if they wanted to. I do not take a stand on whether it is right or wrong to sustain a life on these machines, but I will point out the following:

As I have stated earlier, there is a time for the opening and closing of life. I do believe that when the time is right for the spirit to withdraw from the body, it will. Science cannot stop the great universal time clock, as much as it thinks it could, or no matter how hard it tries. Once again, I believe a soul attempts to experience every situation it possibly can. By being attached to a lifesaving machine, a soul may be in effect helping science in some

way to discover yet another great invention for future genera-
tions—not only medically but perhaps in other ways as well. We
must look at such a situation from a soul point of view. Perhaps a
soul made an agreement before its incarnation to go through
such an experience. It could be a situation that assists family
members and friends in lessons of love and compassion. Let's not
forget that a soul has certain lessons to learn about receiving love
or appreciating the sanctity of life.

Like any moral judgment, each soul has to make this type of
decision on its own. For once again I will say, each soul is unique,
and each has different spiritual needs and must experience what
is best for its soul's growth. There are no right or wrong answers.
It is not our job to judge the decisions of others in these matters
but to consider the experience and lesson from a spiritual point of
view.

CHAPTER 8

Loving Reunions

I personally believe the most crucial aspect of my work is to dispel the power we give to the emotion of fear. Fear is not only an illusion but the largest block to personal growth and the potential of the human spirit to excel. Fear binds people to inner conflict and deprives them of a sense of individual freedom. By being *in fear*, we cannot live *in love*, and indirectly we say good-bye to a lifestyle rich in creativity and productiveness.

Fear is like a vicious circle: When we tune into it, we give it life, then we attract the very thing we fear, and consequently the fear becomes our reality. In other words, the old adage *What you fear comes upon you* is true. We must remember that our thoughts create. Thought is God's energy or creativity. We can use this energy any way we please because we have free will. We must also realize that we are responsible for the results of our thoughts. When we persist in thinking a certain way, such as *in fear*, such thought energy takes shape in our life.

When I begin the process of reading my clients psychically, I inform them of the way they allow fear to enter into their minds and how their fears affect their bodies, their overall health, and their lives in general. As simply as possible, I help them to recognize this adversary and to find ways in which they can change the beliefs that lead to their fears. If they truly get it, they access an enormous number of creative possibilities within themselves.

At first, it is very difficult. People are not likely to change so quickly, especially after decades of conditioning by their families, society, and religious control. But, if anything, I am able to plant a seed and enlighten them to see all the possibilities. By opening a new door in their thinking, I can steer them to use their thoughts in positive and loving ways.

One of the biggest fears is the fear of loss. To some, this fear appears as an impossibility to acknowledge any happiness, goodness, or abundance in their lives. To those who have everything they have always wanted, they might feel on some level that they don't deserve happiness or are not worthy of abundance. Others cannot even imagine a life of fullness and joy because *it is too good to be true.* They think that something will go wrong, and it usually does. I often tell my clients to remember that we are made from the Light. The Light is all-encompassing, always creative, and always bountiful. Even though one does not see the Light, we must believe that through God (Light) anything is possible. God always says *yes*; we are the ones who say *no!*

Included in this fear of loss is the fear of death. I definitely believe (and this may go back to my psychology classes on Freud) that unconsciously the desire and instinct to stay alive is the strongest. Many of us are primarily ego-based and do not want to even acknowledge an end to life, and therefore we fear death. This fear results from the fact that death is a condition over which we have no control. Death is the absolute unknown. It is beyond our human senses and rational, logical thinking. We fear the unknown because we don't know what to expect. We not only don't know what to expect of death, but where, if anyplace, we go. It is unfortunate that death is the ultimate news story because it is this kind of scary thinking, constantly shaped by our society's primitive view of death, that reinforces our fear.

It is amazing to me that so many people still believe that when we die, we cease to exist. I feel the work I do is valuable in dissolving such a view and in opening people's minds to something beyond their physical senses. The moment I relay a spirit message to a loved one, a person's life is usually changed forever. As I look back over the years, I wish I could have captured these incredible experiences on videotape. It is difficult to relate people's reactions in words—it's just not the same as watching them in person in all their glory. With this book, I have attempted to share with you some of that feeling. When a connection between the two worlds—physical and spiritual—has been bridged, nothing short of a miraculous reunion occurs.

It is quite understandable that people are nervous when they come to me. It is more than likely their first experience with a spiritualist, and they have nothing on which to base the experience, except the little they might have read or the inaccurate accounts they may have seen in movies or on television. When I sit with clients who are nervous and anticipatory, I have to establish right from the beginning that spirits use *their* energy as well as mine. I inform them that the energy is very much like an electrical current, and if they are nervous, it will send a wave, or rippling effect, through this electrical line, and the thoughts will come through to me as gibberish. The calmer they are, the better the connection and the easier it is for me to discern a spirit's thoughts. The most important thing for me is to gain some kind of trust from my clients. When I begin to tell clients something about themselves that no one else knows, they realize I am legitimate and their defenses begin to come down. Then I am able to move forward, open the door to spirit, and introduce them to the unknown.

A séance might start with my *picking up* a name or a distinctive personality trait, or my describing the spirit I see. It might be as easy as my saying: "I have your father here, and he is telling me he died of a heart attack." The moment an individual recognizes the information and its spirit source, the entire energy of the room is transformed. A reunion has begun, and a feeling of excitement fills the air. For the client, there is not only a mental change but a physical one as well—eyes widen, mouth drops open, beads of perspiration form on the person's forehead, and the heartbeat quickens. By this time, the client wants to hear more and begins to speak directly to the spirit. Usually I have to ask the person to hold back and calm down because the spirit is trying very hard to concentrate a thought to me, and any undue excitement can affect the signal.

Besides noticeable exhilaration, clients also feel emotional and most often begin to cry. The crying is a mixture of sadness, extreme pleasure, happiness, and relief. As I convey actual mannerisms and inflections to them, the realization hits that a loved one is indeed *not dead*! In addition, they actually *feel the love* pouring into the room from spirit. As detailed messages continue to come through, any "Doubting Thomas" in the group discards his skepticism and becomes hopeful. A grieving appearance soon transforms into one of pure joy, bliss, and contentment. Moreover, the evidential messages serve as proof that a world beyond the grave does exist, and it leaves a rather profound effect on everyone.

When a reunion between the living and the dead takes place, it may be the first time the living understand that death has not robbed them of the love they once experienced with family and friends on the earth plane. Instead, they know that their loved ones are still with them and take a keen interest in their everyday affairs. The living also feel at peace, knowing that their loved ones will meet them when it is their turn to pass into spirit. They also realize they can no longer live life the same way, for they have felt the love and have heard the testimony from the other side, and what was once unknown is no longer. With the knowledge of *no death*, they are free to live life. In an instant, a life overwrought with grief becomes a life ready to live each day and each moment with *newness*.

With a new awareness, the living recognize that they have their own important contribution to make on this earth, and no longer do they want to waste the precious time they have remaining. They also begin to look at life with the knowledge that we are all one and what affects one person affects everyone. They begin to consider every thought and every action with a pronounced responsibility because they know, through their loved ones, that they will *meet up* with their actions in the spirit world. Further, my clients have been informed from their spirit relatives that earth is not the only place for reunions. They, too, have experienced reunions with old family members, friends, and classmates. After years of separation, they reconnect with long-lost loved ones on the other side, where love goes on forever and ever.

In other words, no one will ever be alone.

Happy Anniversary

One of the more moving reunions occurred several years ago. It involved yet another solid, loving relationship between two people. I received a phone call from a man by the name of Larry Gray. He was in his late seventies and spoke in a deep theatrical voice combined with a genteel manner. He said he heard about me from a friend and was wondering if I could help him to do "something special." I asked, "What is it?" He told me his fiftieth wedding anniversary was coming up, and "I want to celebrate it with my wife." The only obstacle was that she was dead. I told him it could be arranged, and we set up the date and time.

The scheduled day for our meeting arrived, and at 12:30 P.M. the doorbell rang. I opened it, and there stood Larry Gray, six foot four, wearing a nicely tailored seventies-style brown suit. I took one look at him and couldn't help but think, *What a sweet person.*

Larry spoke first. "Hello, I'm not bothering you, am I?"

"No, not at all. You must be Larry Gray."

"Yes, yes I am. I hope I'm not late or keeping you from anything?"

Larry had a way of apologizing for every action. It seemed as if he did not want to hurt anyone or get in anyone's way.

"No, not at all, Larry, I've been expecting you. Please come in."

I ushered him into my meeting room and gave him a seat on the couch. He began to talk once again, and I realized that Larry loved to talk a lot. I had to interrupt him, or we would not have had time for the session. I told him this, and he very politely said, "Oh, I'm so sorry. You know I'm an old man, and men like me like to talk. Sorry. Of course, you should do most of the speaking. That's why I'm here, isn't it?" Larry let out a chuckle.

I sat down and explained how I did my work. I uttered my opening prayer, and when it was completed, I looked to Larry's right, and I saw a beautiful brunette dressed in a forties sort of way. I told him, "I believe Kay is standing to the side of you wearing a light pink dress. She reminds me so much of an actress."

"That's because she was an actress. We met acting in Berkeley," replied Larry.

I continued. "She calls you *Love*. She says *Love* instead of your name."

"That's nice. We called each other many things. Gee, I look so old. I have gray hair now."

"She said she married your heart, not your hair." We both laughed, and then I continued.

"Kay says you have a beautiful voice. She says you sing all the time."

"Yes, that's true. Every weekend I go down to the Christian Science Church and sing in the choir. It gives me something to do. They are very nice to me there."

"She is talking now about your wedding. Did you get married outside of California, like New York?"

"Yes, New York City. Can she give you the year?"

"I believe she is telling me 1940."

"Yes, that's right. What about the church? Will she give you the name of the church?"

"Let's see." I waited for a few minutes, and all I got was something about an actors' church.

Larry responded, "Well, the church was right around the corner and the actors from all the theaters would go there. Will she tell you where we lived?"

I sent this mental question to his wife, and after a few moments I said, "She is saying something about uptown. Like Upper West Side in a very small apartment."

"Oh, that's good, that's good. Yes. It was known as Washington Heights. Gee, this gives me a thrill."

"Larry, she is mentioning something about Philadelphia. Were there any ties to Philadelphia?"

"Yes."

"Because she is talking about going down to Philadelphia on the train. Were there relatives in Philadelphia? Do you understand?"

"Yes."

"It was about the same time as your wedding. You were living in New York, and you went down to Philadelphia?"

"After we were married, I had to go to Philadelphia every Sunday for a while until I left my church there and got one in New York."

I began to laugh and clap, "That's good. That's good. Okay, hold on, let's see what else.

"Kay is telling me she was alone when she died, and she wanted it that way. Please don't be upset about it."

"Yes, I was very upset about that, Kay. For goodness sake, you could have waited."

"No, she had to go when it was right. She is such a sweet woman. She is wearing a beautiful hat. It looks like something from the forties. She is telling me she used to love to wear hats, and would often say to you, I'm going downtown to buy a hat."

"Yes, that's exactly right. Gee, that was some time ago. But Kay loved her hats. My, she had quite a beautiful collection. She always dressed so nice. She loved color, and beautiful things."

"She still does. She is going on about a piano."

Larry began laughing and insisted that Kay continue to tell me about the piano.

"She tells me you have the piano at home, and she used to love to play it. She played it all the time. She also mentions something to do with Wagner. Do you understand this?"

"Yes, I do. It's amazing! I bought a piano for Kay, and it is still sitting in the house. But I played it, she never did. I used to play and she would sing with me. We had quite an arrangement going on. Do you remember that, Kay? Oh, yes, I still play it. Does she see me playing?"

"She does see you playing the piano and stands in the same spot off to the left, just like she used to. What is this about Wagner?" I asked Larry.

"Well, gee, I am ashamed to say this, but I love to collect old records. I have quite a big assortment. I particularly love classical music and just recently was playing Wagner on the phonograph. Maybe it's crazy, but I let it play all day. It's relaxing. I guess it's all right; it doesn't hurt anyone."

I returned, "No, just the needle," and we both had a nice chuckle. I proceeded with the rest of the message.

"Larry, Kay wants you to know she was with you at the graveyard earlier."

"Well, today is our anniversary, and I wanted her to know I love her and was thinking about her. So you know that, Kay?"

"Yes, she is very pleased that you were there. She loves the roses that you brought to the cemetery."

"Oh, that was nothing. I thought she would like them."

"She did," I continued. "She is showing me a crypt. Is she in a crypt, please?"

"Yes, she is, and I will be right next to her."

"She is showing you with the flowers. Funny, she is putting a pole in your hand. I don't know what this means. Do you understand this?"

"Well, I think so. When I went to the cemetery to see her, I had to grab a pole to put the flowers in front of her crypt. Her place is way up. Could that be what she is speaking of?"

"Yes, that is it. And she talks about all the way up." Kay began sending me another message very quickly. I looked up and replied to her, "Got it . . . got it . . . thank you." Then I turned to Larry. "Is the location of her resting place in the back? It's kind of screwy, the way you have to get to this place. It's in the back, down some marble stairs, and to the side. She is telling me all about this."

Larry was not sure. In trying to decipher Kay's message, I did a

good job of totally mixing myself up in the maze and Larry as well.
I proceeded.

"There is a lady standing next to Kay. She has a very distinctive
voice. Very theatrical. I believe she also sang opera. She brings up
the piano again. Do you know why?"

"Yes, of course. That is Esther. She was an incredible singer.
All three of us used to work together in the theater. She also was
my piano teacher for years. Oh, golly, how nice to hear from her."

"This lady wants me to tell you that there is a big theater community over there. A lot of voice coaches and music teachers. It's
different though, she says. Music isn't as it is on earth. It's more
undiluted. She says, here we have pure harmony. On the earth,
you just talk about it, but it doesn't come close to the truth."

"Beautiful."

The reading lasted for some time with his wife and teacher as
they relived memories of bygone days shared on the earth. It was
such a beautiful fiftieth anniversary. I thought, *What else could
she say to top this?* And then she said it.

"Larry, do you know anything about Paris? I mean, did you and
Kay spend time there?"

"Yes, as a matter of fact we did. What is she saying about it?"

"She wants me to mention something about standing on the
Eiffel Tower in Paris. That this was one of the happiest times of
her life. Do you understand what she is referring to?"

Larry started to cry. He took out a tissue, wiped his eyes,
and looked straight ahead at me. "It was one of the happiest
days of my life, too. That was how we spent the first day on our
honeymoon."

I added, "Kay says the rest of your life together was a
honeymoon."

Larry smiled, and I continued with her message.

"She will always be with you, Larry, and . . . hold on, she says that
she wants you to go home and play her a love song on the piano."

With that, Larry smiled and said, "Boy, that's Kay, all right. She
doesn't know when to stop."

And I told him, "She never will."

Charlie

Much of the richness of my work is measured by the situations I encounter among people who love one another very much. That was the way I looked at it until the time I received a phone call, and the operator said a deaf woman was on the phone and wanted to speak to me. I said, "Okay," and the operator translated our conversation. The lady's name was Susan, and she was very depressed and requested a reading. She wanted to know if it could be worked out. I told the operator yes, and a date was set.

On the day of the reading, I wasn't sure if anything would transpire. At eleven o'clock the doorbell rang. Two women were waiting—one rather thin in stature, with dark hair; the other was a little larger and had red hair. The thin woman introduced herself as Kathy and told me she was the interpreter.

I invited them in and offered them some water to drink. "I hope you didn't have a hard time trying to find the place," I said. I looked behind me and saw Kathy busy signing to Susan. When we moved into the séance room, we agreed that it would be best for Susan to sit in front of me, and Kathy to stand behind me and sign to Susan.

I began my introduction by explaining the process of spirit communication. As a native New Yorker I speak rather quickly, but Kathy kept up with me all the way. I was amazed how quickly she could spell out what I said. As I recall this situation, I remember how I felt, especially about the love and healing Kathy brought to her work. I was amazed with her interpreting abilities as she was with mine.

I began Susan's reading by performing a psychic chart on her. When I do someone's psychic chart, I usually hold a pad and pen, tune into an individual's energy pattern, and write or draw my impressions. Sometimes, I do it at the beginning of a session to ease into the communication of a reading. If I give an individual some correct psychic information about herself, she knows right away that I am legitimate. Any wall of doubt is removed, and the communication process with spirits is much easier. Susan seemed to be very much a loner, and one who could be very stubborn. I described her family, one that wasn't very communicative and open, and relayed that her deafness was due to the two small bones in her ears that were not fully developed when she was born. She acknowledged that I was correct and was quite happy that I was able to give her such specific information. After finishing her chart, I said my prayer and began my opening-up process. I immediately began to receive information about her home.

"This is quite strange, but I am shown what I believe to be your house. Do you have a brownish sofa under a window with a colored blanket or quilt on top of it?"

After the exchange of interpretation, Kathy gave me Susan's answer. "Yes, that is right. It is right under the window, and the blanket is on the couch but not all the time."

I must say it was quite different receiving the feedback from someone standing behind me, even an interpreter.

I continued. "There are several pictures on a metal stand to the right of the couch. I also see what appears to be plastic or silk flowers on this shelf as well. Do you accept this?"

"Yes, that is exactly right."

"I am also shown an orange carpet. It is worn in a couple of spots, especially near a door. I believe this to be the front door to your apartment. I am also shown a kitchen. Hold on. I don't know who is giving me this information. Let me ask."

I mentally asked the spirit to identify itself. There was no response, so I sat very quietly. I was then shown many pictures on a refrigerator and described them to Susan. "I am shown so many pictures on the refrigerator. There are many of a dog."

Susan started to laugh. She told me that they were pictures of her dog. As I continued, I suddenly felt an incredible amount of love fill the room. It was a love that seemed so noble and unconditional. Then I blurted out . . . "Charlie."

With that, Susan began to cry hysterically. I was totally at a loss and stared at her, waiting to hear a reply or an explanation. I obviously hit a nerve and wanted to know what it was.

Kathy spoke for Susan. "Yes! Charlie was my dog. Charlie is

the one I came here to contact. He died two months ago, and I miss him very much."

I could hardly believe what I was hearing. I realized why I was having trouble identifying a person. It became obvious that the information was *from the dog*! The dog was showing me things that he understood.

Susan was busy signing until Kathy finally spoke. "Susie is telling us that Charlie loved to sit on the couch all the time, and that his favorite place was the blanket. From time to time he would also claw at the carpet in front of the door and pretend he was burying something."

"I understand. I thought it strange to see the visions from a low angle, but now I understand why. I am seeing them through Charlie's eyes."

After a moment I continued the reading. "Charlie gives you lots of love. He is showing me a red light and tells me he did something with this red light."

Susan was extremely excited as she signed feverishly to Kathy. "Yes, it was the light that would let me know the phone was ringing. Charlie would come over and nudge me when he would see it. He was great! He had very human qualities."

"He is giving a thought that he had a pretty red collar with jewels . . . well, they look like diamonds. I'm sure they are not real diamonds."

Susan laughed and told us that they weren't real but that they did shine. She said it would rile her when people made fun of Charlie because he wore such a "feminine collar."

After a giggle, I continued. "Charlie is describing how you would walk him down to the corner store to buy some bread and milk."

"Yes, that is right."

Then I started to laugh. Charlie had sent me a very funny thought, and I relayed his message.

"Charlie is telling me that he didn't like the baths in the sink."

"Yes. Every Friday night I would give him a bath, and you're right, he didn't like it one bit. He would fight me all the time. I think after a while, he got used to it. Can I ask you a question?"

"Yes, of course."

Susan slowly began to cry and started to sign a question. "Was Charlie in a lot of pain when he died? And can you please tell him I'm sorry."

I asked, "Did Charlie have trouble with his legs at one point? I mean, was he unable to walk? Because I feel pain in the right side."

"Not until the very end. He was on medication."

"Do you know if he had diabetes?"

"Yes, he did. He also had kidney problems. Is he telling you that?"

"Yes, he is giving me the thought of what was wrong with him before his death. He is also telling me he loves you very much and that you helped him. Did you put him to sleep?"

"Yes, but I didn't want to."

"Your dog was in a lot of pain in the end. You really helped him. Do you know that?"

Susan did not answer. She bent her head and shook it up and down.

"Charlie still sleeps with you at the end of the bed. Does that make sense?"

"Yes. He would always come on the bed in the middle of the night. I would wake up and find his head on the pillow next to me."

"Do you know someone with a name like Ivy? I know it is a strange name, but I feel this is the name?"

Susan began to think but could not place the name. Then a few minutes later she burst out: "Yes! I was speaking to her on the phone last week. She is helping me to get another dog. It is very hard to find a dog for the hearing impaired, and she told me she might have one for me."

"I am getting a very strong vibration or sensation from this animal that you will get the other dog, and you won't be alone much longer. Charlie says he will help and make sure the other dog knows what to do. By the way, he shows me a white dog. It almost looks like a husky."

Susan got very excited. "That is the type of dog Ivy is trying to get for me."

"You will have it, don't worry. Charlie tells me you will never be alone!"

With that, we thanked the spirit world for their assistance, and I asked them to help Susan on her path.

As I said earlier in the book, animals survive death. When animals pass into the world of spirit, they accept their transition very much as a natural occurrence. We could certainly learn from them. I have often been asked, "Where does my loving pet go?" Our pets also go to a heaven world. They go to a very beautiful, physical type of world—the same place occupied by humans. When an animal passes, it is met by the human being(s) with whom it had a rapport while on earth. If no one is available, or if an animal didn't share its earth experience with a human, it is often met by animal caretakers. These keepers are generous, loving souls who watch over our pets until a family member with strong love ties to the pet joins it in the spirit world. More than likely, animal caretakers are people who adored animals on earth.

It is fairly common for your newly departed animal to come back to its earthly place of residence. More than likely it will sit on the same chair, sleep in the same spot, and watch you very closely. It remembers the kindness and love it received from you on the earth, and it will often return to watch over and protect you.

So please, don't ever take an animal, or any other form of life, for granted. We are here to share in the mystery of a divine plan of love for all of God's creatures.

Alzheimer's Disease

Dying a slow and debilitating death from Alzheimer's disease is not only undignified but at times almost inhuman. Yet, each year hundreds of thousands get this lingering disease. Alzheimer's disease is a condition in which nerve cells degenerate in the brain, and the brain substance shrinks. The disease is accompanied by forgetfulness, or memory loss, and a disorientation of time and place. In the final stages, a person might suffer from severe psychosis, including delusions and paranoia.

Even though the cause for the disease is still up in the air, there are several theories: Some believe it to be genetic; others believe environmental factors, such as leads or metals, play a part. One thing is for sure. As the elderly population increases, the strain on families and the medical community will also increase. I do hope that more can be studied and conclusions can be drawn to bring an end to this devastating affliction.

People have asked me many questions about friends and family members with Alzheimer's, such as: *Can they hear me? Do they see me? Where are they? Are they still here? Are they dead? Has the soul left the body? Can the soul go on? What is the story?*

I had a meeting one day with a charming woman by the name of Sydelle. She was referred by a close friend. At the beginning of the reading she mentioned that her father died and that she needed to resolve certain issues. She particularly wanted to know if he was at peace.

When we started the session, I first got a very strong sense that Sydelle was very nervous and unsure, not only about the reading but of her own future. Many questions seemed to be dancing around her head. I assured her that hopefully her fears and anxieties would be eliminated by our communication with spirit. I started to get in tune with her energy. Immediately, I picked up that there was a little bit of hostility between her and her mother.

"Sydelle, are you speaking with your mother?"

"Yes, I speak to her."

"I don't mean to pry, but I get a sense that you and she are not quite together."

"I'm not sure I know what you mean."

"It feels like she seems to be a burden to you sometimes, and you lose patience with her."

"Oh, yes. That is true. I have a hard time telling her anything."

The session shifted, and I felt a door of some sort open behind me, and suddenly an onslaught of people came through.

"All at once I feel as though this room is full. Hold on . . . let me tune into who's here." I closed my eyes and saw the figure of a gentleman. He stood very straight and had a serious expression. He gave me a feeling of being *out of it*.

"Sydelle, I believe I have your father here. I feel there was something wrong with his head before he died because he gives me the distinct impression that his head area was affected. I also get a sense that he was in a hospital or convalescent home for a long time. Was he bedridden for a long time?"

"Yes, my dad had Alzheimer's for thirteen years."

"Oh, my God, that's why I feel so out of it. He can't believe it all. I have to say, he still doesn't feel as though he is fully acclimated to things. I mean, he looks around and has such a sense of unbelief."

"Well, I don't think he believed in this sort of thing."

"Could be, but . . . Your father wants to thank you for lighting the candle. Does that make sense?"

"Yes, I lit some candles while he was sick to help him move on to the other side."

"He wants to thank you for this, along with all the prayers. They helped him so much. He says he is still confused, but slowly he is beginning to figure things out. Was his funeral at a temple?"

"Yes."

"He was there. He says he saw all of you. But he was a bit surprised about the number of people. He said he expected twice the number."

"He had so many friends, but because he was away from life for so long, he didn't have many friends left."

"Who is Jack?"

"That's him, that's his name."

"He is mentioning an African blanket and something about pictures. He saw all the pictures. Did you display some pictures of your father? Pictures of him throughout his life?"

"Yes, that's correct. At his funeral, I arranged one of his African blankets and placed pictures of him on top of it. I wanted it to be a collage of my father's life."

"Who is Rose?"

"His mother."

"He wants you to know that Rose came to greet him when he passed. He had not seen her for a long time. Is that right?"

"She died when he was a child."

"She's a funny one. Do you know that she watches you in the kitchen? She also loves the type of clothes you wear. She is showing me flowing dresses."

Sydelle laughs out loud and thanks me for bringing in her grandmother. "I never knew her, but I am happy that she is around me."

Jack began to speak again, and I continued with the messages. "Your father mentions the name of Mark and says he helps him out."

"Mark is my brother. That is so interesting because Mark took over my father's business after my father died."

"Do you know if Mark has Jack's cuff links or tie clips?"

"Yes, he wears my father's cuff links."

"Do you know about him sitting in an office with awards and commendations on the wall?"

"Yes, he is in my father's office, and it is exactly as my father left it. The awards are for best salesman. They are on the wall behind the desk."

"Your father shows me his dark green chair. It is the one your brother sits on in the office. Please ask him if there is a slight tear or rip on the seat. I believe it would be on the right side, under his leg when he sits down."

"That sounds very strange. But, you know what? Mark mentioned that he had to get a new chair because the old one is worn. I don't know if it has a rip, but I will be sure to ask him. That is just amazing."

It is rare that clients will ask for business advice from the other side. I do inform them that the spirit world does not necessarily have knowledge of how things will be. As I said before, far too many factors are involved, including karmic law. I tell my clients, "We can ask the spirit, but please know that you have to make your own decisions. It is not the spirit's responsibility to tell you how to run your life or your business affairs."

I informed Sydelle of the same, and she replied that she welcomed her father's advice since the business was originally his. "I feel confident that he will give me sound business advice."

I told her what I was receiving. "Do you know if your brother has been considering acquiring a partner?"

"I'm not sure, but I will ask him."

"All right. He is telling me it has been very tough to make money from this business. It seems rough. But, he said, you will have to wait it out because it will change, and eventually you will be selling this business."

Sydelle let out a gasp. She said they had no intention of selling their business. If anything, they planned on keeping it in the family for as long as possible.

"Your father says he worried too much about his business, and it took up all of his life. He doesn't want you to get into the same mode. He wishes he had more time on earth to do other things than work. He thinks he could have done a lot more if he gave himself the time. He was rigid and demanding about work. He wanted to get things done to prove himself. He says you could have taught him a lot. You teach him a lot now."

Sydelle became very emotional, as did her father. Then he mentioned Sydelle's mother.

"He is worried about your mother. He is telling me they argued too much. Part of him still loves her, and he is more understanding of her. She is not happy with herself. She expects the world to do things for her. You have to live your own life. Point that out to her."

"I will."

I asked Sydelle if she had any questions for her father. Her question helped me to change my thinking about people who suffer from Alzheimer's.

"Where was my father during the time he had Alzheimer's? I mean, where was his spirit? Did it die and go somewhere else?"

"Your father finds your question interesting and said he will try and answer it as best as he can. There is such a difference in understanding between the earth world and the heaven worlds. He mentions that most of the time he was unaware and felt he was in some sort of a light sleep. He does mention that there were distinct times when he was out of his body and what he believed to be his spirit was looking at his body on the bed and the people in the room. It was difficult for him because he had no sense of time as we know it. He didn't have full awareness of time and space as we have on the earth."

"Did he see spirit forms around him?"

"He kind of sensed some energies around him, but not until he passed over did he know who these people were. He says a father figure and Rose came to get him."

I told Sydelle that many others in the spirit world who have had Alzheimer's disease have given similar answers. Some didn't realize where they were. Some were totally asleep during the whole experience. Others were often out of their bodies and very aware of their families, and many times had attempted to give them messages.

She pressed further. "Why did he have to go through this disease?"

"He doesn't think you will understand it exactly, but believe it or not, he chose it before coming to earth. He is telling me he had to go through the experience to equal things out."

I then added my understanding of the situation: Many times a spirit has to go through some disease to overcome it to become strong, and to break the link so that a disease will burn out of the family line.

After that session many years ago, Sydelle and I became good friends. Every few months she calls to see how I am doing, and she very recently informed me: "I don't know if you remember this, but in one of your first readings with me, I asked my dad about the business. He said that we would find a partner and eventually sell it. I just wanted to tell you that my brother got a partner a few months ago, and right now, he is signing the papers to sell the dealership."

Tell It from the Mountain

This next session is one of the most recognized in my career. A year after the session, the news got out about the incredible details that came through, and the NBC show *Unsolved Mysteries* wanted to recreate the session. A few months later, auditions were held to find someone who looked like me. A few months after that, the show was taped. Since that show was taped two years ago, it has become one of the most popular episodes in all of *Unsolved Mysteries* history and can be seen often on the Lifetime cable channel. It is one of my most memorable sessions.

It was June of 1995, and I was sitting outside of my apartment waiting for my next client. I checked my schedule, but I did not recognize the names of my six o'clock appointment—Don and Sue Raskin. At five minutes to six, a couple came walking down the path. I remember my first reaction when I saw them. The gentleman did not look well. He actually looked quite ill, and I thought the lady with him was his daughter, but it turned out to be his wife.

After saying my prayer, I immediately noticed that several spirits were surrounding me. I picked up many who were female and some very strong male energies. I began to relay my sensations and observations, hoping that the present spirits were indeed the person or persons to whom they wanted to communicate.

"I must tell you that when you walked through the door, there was a young man standing behind you, Don. He seems young when he passes. Do you have a son in spirit?"

They stared at each other in amazement, and ever so slowly, he looked over at me and acknowledged that this was true.

"Yes."

"He says he loves you very, very much and that you have nothing to be afraid of. He really loves you. Love you. He keeps saying that to me. Does the initial *A* mean something to you? Did he know anyone named Adam?"

"I don't think so," responded Sue.

I looked over at Doug and told him about his mother and father. "Your son says your mom and dad are here tonight. They come in holding hands with your boy. Do you know the initial *M*?"

"Yes, that is my father. Mike is his name," Doug replied.

"I also have a lady here with a name like Lillie, Millie, or Ellie."

Sue jumped in. "That's my sister. She also died."

"Did they also call her Babs?"

"Yes, among other things."

"Your sister is very funny. She and your father are cracking up together. They get along well. But your son wants to speak. He says he is the guest of honor tonight. Was he in a hospital?"

"Yes."

"He says he was very uncomfortable. Was this a big surprise? He says people were shocked. He says this was very unexpected. This seems like some kind of an accident. Were there head injuries?"

"Yes, that is right."

The Raskins grabbed each other's hands and held one another tightly.

"He gives me a pain in the head. I also think his neck was affected. Did he spend any time in a helicopter? Because he knows about the helicopter ride."

"Yes. He was flown by helicopter to the hospital."

"He gives me a very strong sense of climbing. He is showing me a mountain. I also feel a sense of slipping or falling. Do you understand?"

They both started to cry and acknowledged that the information was correct.

I continued. "He says he always knew something like this was going to happen to him. He always lived on the edge. There was nothing you could have done. Stop feeling guilty about it because you could not have stopped him. Did he ever think about sky-diving? He is showing me sky-diving. He says if he didn't go from climbing a mountain, he would have died from sky-diving."

Don spoke up. "He was always adventurous. Always doing one thing or another."

"Did he like photography? He says he has taken pictures from all over the world. He knows you were looking through his books. He says there isn't one picture you could find in his books to describe where he is. The colors of the sky . . . It's so rich with colors. Indescribable! Light violets and pinks. Don't worry about me, he says. I'm in a big adventure over here. Who's Tam or Tammy?"

"That's his sister."

"Would you tell her that he loves her and thanks her for all her good wishes, good thoughts, good prayers, and her love. It means a lot!"

"Yes, we will be sure to."

"Did his niece write him a letter or card?"

Doug responded, "Yes, I think so. At the funeral."

"Your son loved it, please tell her. He is also mentioning someone with the name of Mark. Did he know someone with this name?"

"Yes, that was his good friend."

"Hello to him from Doug. Please tell him that he'll always be around him, and they will always remain good friends."

I then looked over at Don, who did not look so well. I realized that his grief had taken over his life, and he looked like nothing more than an empty shell. I conveyed his son's concern about his health.

"Don, Doug says to be careful about getting an ulcer. He says you're having trouble sleeping. Have you been to the doctor about this?"

"Yes, just last week. He gave me a prescription for some sleeping pills."

"He wants to tell you both that you helped him live his life to the fullest. You always supported him. You always believed in him. You're the best. You're the best, he says. Was there a picture of him at the service?"

"Yes."

"He is showing me a board with many pictures on it, and in

the middle is one big picture. He says you had trouble finding that one main picture."

They both began to laugh, and then Sue spoke up. "We looked all over for the main one. We had many pictures of Doug on his various trips."

"He saw how full the place was and hoped you didn't go to too much trouble."

"We wanted to. It was a celebration of his life."

"Doug is telling me you picked out music for the service. He tells me it had a Scottish or Irish feel, like Enya."

"Enya is exactly what we used!" said Sue.

I looked over at Don, as Doug addressed the next question to him.

"Don, do you usually exercise? Because Doug is showing me a horse. Why don't the two of you go and enjoy some horseback riding together?"

Don answered, "My best friend and I are going. This is the shirt Doug gave me to wear."

"Enjoy it, Dad. Please enjoy yourself for me. Just enjoy yourself."

At that point a very intriguing question came through, and the response to this day still amazes me.

"Did you have a picture of him duplicated or repro-duced? He's laughing about that picture as if it is an inside joke or something."

"The picture was taken when we were on a trip with Doug. Our daughter spotted a flash of light in the middle of the photo-graph that looked like a puff of smoke in the shape of a heart. She could see the words *I love you* in the heart. She had it blown up!"

"He says, I did that. He's laughing about it. Do you under-stand? It was me. It was my gift to you. Think of it as a postcard from heaven."

This last bit of information demonstrated once again the power of love to transcend even the physical. The remainder of the séance brought through Don's mother and father and his Aunt Bea. Each described in detail how they knew Don as a young child. Then Doug came in and spoke until the end of the session, and with each thought, he brought forward amazing proof of life after death.

I asked Sue, "Were you cutting out newspaper articles with scissors?"

"Yes."

"They were all standing around watching you cut them out. When was that?"

"Last week. There was a big article about Doug in the paper, about his death. It wasn't just an obituary, it was about Mount Fuji."

"Are you going to have a scrapbook or memorial book of some sort? He says you're getting all the pieces together, but you haven't glued them in yet. You stuck them there. He knows about that."

They both smiled, and I continued.

"Kieto. What does that mean?"

"It's in Japan, very near to where the accident happened. We were with him in Kieto."

"Did he have a bike, a mountain bike? Do you know about the bike?"

"We're having the bike sent home to us."

"He is mentioning how much he liked the picture that was taken of him at the base of Mount Fuji. Do you have this?"

"Well, there are pictures being developed by the climbing team that we haven't gotten yet."

"Would you please remember this?"

"Yes, of course."

The meeting lasted another quarter of an hour. The Raskins left my house feeling very differently than when they arrived. The look on Don's face was a sure sign that he had started on the road to recovery. They knew not only that their son was still alive but that he was around them all the time.

I found out later that Doug Raskin was not just an ordinary son. He seemed to be an angel from heaven. He spent several years traveling to foreign countries and aiding the poor. He even swam through rough waters with food strapped on his back so he could feed the poor. He was adventurous and caring, and anyone whose life he touched certainly felt his light.

About two months after the initial reading, the phone rang, and it was Sue Raskin. She told me she just received the mail. Doug's climbing team had sent photographs. She said, "The first picture I pulled out was that of Doug grinning from ear to ear as he stood at the base of Mount Fuji."

·SECTION THREE·

THE NEXT STEP

CHAPTER 9

Beyond Grief

There is a time for everything,
and a season for every activity under heaven:
a time to be born and a time to die.
—*ECCLESIASTES 3:1*

Do we ever get over the loss of a loved one? Is it possible to start life anew without our dear one sharing it with us? Will our memories of pleasant times together help us get our lives back?

There are no easy answers to these questions. Once someone passes out of the world of the physical and into the world of the spiritual, we can never physically experience them again the way we once knew. But we can always experience them and have them share in our lives by keeping their memories alive in our minds and hearts and by realizing that, as spiritual beings not limited to physical properties, they are more often around us than ever before.

As the Bible quote says, there is a natural time and place for every occurrence or experience on this earth. Each time we come back to the physical world, we go through a growth experience of the soul. Every occurrence in our lives determines and measures our growth. Like the cycle of the seasons when something dies in the winter to be born again in the spring, it is impossible to have life without an ending and a new beginning. Everything we do is about growth.

To this end, every living creature on this planet experiences loss in one way or another. It may be a loss of a job, or a loss through a divorce, an accident, or a crime. It may be an unrealized goal, or just growing older. We might consider these losses as distressing life changes, but we often find that these, too, have their time and place in our lives. In order to experience a loss and transform it, there are steps we can take to start on the successful road to a healthier, fuller, and more centered life. The first of these steps is to recognize and deal with our grief.

How to Recognize Grief

Grief has many appearances—physical, mental, and emotional. Helplessness, anxiety, sleeplessness, fear, despair, irritability, anger, depression, nausea, shortness of breath, heart palpitations, even thoughts of suicide can all be considered symptoms or signs of grief. It is important to realize that grieving over the loss of someone (or even something like a job) is very normal and quite natural. When we grieve, we feel as though our lives are over and that they will never be the same. We feel that we cannot go on even one more day without the person we lost. We feel as if our whole world has turned upside down. Nothing seems to fit or make any kind of sense. We seem to be totally out of balance in every area of our lives. We can't think straight; we can't make decisions correctly. We often find that we cannot control our emotions, or we cry sporadically over the smallest of challenges. All of these feelings are very much a part of the grief experience and should never be dismissed or judged as wrong.

At such a time, it is common for bereaved individuals to have a sense of apathy for their own physical, emotional, and spiritual welfare. It is of the utmost importance for individuals to be able to cope with their grief with the goal of restoring some sense of well-being to their lives.

How do we do this? How do we recover from our grief? Although the focus of this book is the loss of a loved one, the following stages are applicable to any loss—of a person, a pet, a home, a job, or living with a long-term illness. This healing process applies in most situations where we feel at a loss.

1. Shock
When people hear that a loved one has died, their first reaction might be one of shock, or they could experience a sense of numbness, thinking: *This could not have happened.* They might reject the idea that a loss has occurred at all. They look as if they're in a trance, or zombielike, as they shuffle around with little awareness of their surroundings. Later, they may have no memory of the first days of the news of the loss. This memory loss is nature's way of coming to our aid. By shutting down, our minds are unconsciously trying to cope with the sudden change in our lives.

This initial shock might last a few hours or a few days, and once it does wear off, it is important to have a close friend or loved one nearby to assist us in our grief. Often, family and friends are at our side during the funeral, but once it is over, they are gone. It is usually at this time that we come out of shock and need someone the most. For when the shock is over, the real pain begins.

When you are going through the pain, remember that being angry and hurt are natural reactions to a loss. You will get over it. Life will return to somewhat normal circumstances once again.

2. Denial
Whenever we feel hurt, our tendency is to deny it. By doing this, we seem to ease our pain. We so want the hurt not to exist, so by denying our pain, we fool ourselves into thinking it doesn't exist. Again, it is the unconscious part of ourselves trying to cope with loss. Denial can manifest in many ways:

1. We lose interest or stop our involvement in everyday affairs.
2. We sleep too much or suffer from insomnia.

3. We lose our appetite.
4. We don't take interest in our daily hygiene.
5. We become depressed and can't seem to snap out of it.

Once again, it is important for us to understand that denial is a normal stage of the grief process and that we can eventually get beyond it.

3. Just Feel

The first step on the road to healing yourself is to accept the reality of the situation—that you have suffered a loss. The loss is real, and the recognition of it is important. It is normal to feel. Make sure *you feel*! Do not repress your anger, your sadness, your upset, or your helplessness. These feelings are all very natural. Do not cover or hide your feelings, thinking you are immature, or that *this kind of behavior is unacceptable*. If you feel like crying, let it out. Cry! Crying is a natural reaction and is very necessary in healing the body. There is, in fact, scientific proof that tears of sadness are biochemically different from tears of laughter and joy. So crying actually helps you to release certain chemicals from your body.

It is natural that you will often think of your loved one, and in doing so, sometimes anger creeps into your thoughts. If you are angry, allow your anger to come out without hurting yourself or others. Take it out by doing something physical like sports, or punching a pillow, or going to a remote area and screaming to your heart's content. It's understandable that you feel hurt and pain, and letting out your anger in beneficial ways is healthy.

Also, do not qualify the way you *should* feel. We are all individuals, and our relationships with one another are uniquely our own. Therefore, each of us reacts differently to a situation, especially a loss. Don't judge yourself by the way others feel. There is no right or wrong way.

It is also quite common for us to want to get away from the pain as soon as possible, so we may try to medicate ourselves with tranquilizers. Sometimes we might need them as a quick temporary relief. However, drugs hinder our progress in the long run, and the feelings we are trying to repress usually surface in one way or another.

In many of my sessions over the years, I have met hundreds of people, and I can tell immediately when they have not dealt with their feelings of loss. Their bodies show it all, for the outer is a mirror to the inner world. They have repressed their feelings so much that they are very unhealthy. The unprocessed feelings of grief literally eat away at them and manifest in a myriad of health concerns and illnesses, including obesity, allergies, aches, pains, breathing trouble, and, in some cases, cancer.

Therefore, in order to stay healthy, we must fully go through the experience of feeling. Our feelings are our barometer for living.

4. Acknowledgment and Acceptance

Once we have gone through our shock, denial, hurt, pain, and anger, we will progress into a stage of acknowledgment and acceptance of the actual death. This is the first step in bringing back some sort of balance to our lives. Accepting the death of our loved one does not mean that we approve of their death. We are merely seeing the situation realistically. We understand that our loved one has passed on, and we will not see them physically anymore. However, we will see them again when it is our time to pass into the spiritual realms.

A loss is a loss, and there is no way to change it. The amount of pain you might feel will correspond directly to the intensity of your feelings for your deceased loved one. But it is important to realize that by feeling your pain, you are actually healing. You can and will begin to get your strength back, and you will move back into life and continue the learning experiences you are here to learn.

5. Settling Practical Matters

Besides emotionally dealing with a loss, it is also important to establish a sense of order in your daily life from a financial and practical point of view. This is especially true if the deceased handled the money in your relationship. Again, do not be scared to ask for help. A family member or friend may be able to offer some advice in this area, and they may be able to help you a great deal more than you ever thought.

If there are medical or insurance claims, have them taken care of in order to give yourself some peace of mind and financial freedom. The sooner this area is handled, the better you will feel all around. You will also want to research all your finances, make lists, and review all known assets, bank accounts, holdings, and so on. You may also need to create a list of all your expenses, debts, and loans so that the correct payments are allocated for each. You may need to liquidate your assets, if this is an option. In most cases, you will need to inform creditors of the recent death so they can adjust their records accordingly.

This is a time when you will have to take care of all legal matters concerning yourself and the deceased. In order to settle most practical and financial matters, you will need copies of the death certificate. You may also have to contact an attorney if there is an inheritance or an estate to settle.

6. Moving On

When the sun sets, it also rises again. You have been through an incredible emotional period, and at times it seemed unbearable and you did not want to go on any further. However, the time has arrived when you are ready to assess your life and move on. A new chapter in your life has begun.

You are now at a perfect place to seek guidance from a support or grief group. There are many support groups for people who have experienced a specific loss, for example, the loss of a spouse, or a child, or a sibling, or the loss of someone to AIDS, cancer, and the like. The individuals in a support group have also been through a similar loss, and, like you, hurt. Everyone needs help to get their lives going once again. I suggest that you visit a support group meeting and observe. See if you fit in and if you feel comfortable with the other members. Perhaps you might want a friend or family member to accompany you the first time. Above all, don't be afraid to ask for help.

This is a time you may also want to get involved in a physical activity on a regular basis. Join a gym, play tennis or golf, take a daily walk or jog. It is important that you get involved in physical activities so you can keep your mind sharp, your body in tune, and your emotions in balance. Physical activity helps to release anger, clear away depression, and dispatch beneficial hormones throughout your body.

As I have previously pointed out, grieving and healing do not occur overnight, and there is no way of judging the amount of time it will take any individual to personally heal and start a new life. You will always have your loved ones around you, even though you may not be aware of their presence. You can always be happy and joyful with the memories you hold of them. Do not diminish these memories, for they are just as special as they were when the experiences occurred.

Watch for Behavior That Could Lead to Impairment or Injury

It is important to realize that there will be setbacks, so keeping track of feelings and mood swings is necessary. For instance, many people fall back into denial, disbelieving that death has occurred. Certain individuals are not able to come out of their denial and grief, and they may exhibit some sort of self-destructive behavior. Be aware of the following signs. If these signs continue for a long period of time, professional help is needed.

1. An individual may begin to entertain thoughts of suicide. This is common at first, but if a person persists with the actual means of how he or she wants to accomplish this, it is a red flag. Get preventative assistance.
2. A grieving person may need at first to take some medication, such as tranquilizers and mood elevators. Because a

person could easily become dependent on such medication, he or she needs careful monitoring. Sometimes an individual will try to gloss over the pain and trauma he or she is experiencing. A medical professional should be seen on a regular basis. The quicker a person is off medication, the sooner the fog lifts, and the sooner a person will be able to cope with the loss and start the healing process.

3. If an individual stays completely detached from his or her normal activities and starts to obsess, or stays alone in a depressed state for long periods, it's time to seek a professional counselor who deals specifically with grief. A counselor can help to bring such a person back to reality.

Though the grief process is painful, it is a part of the experience of life that we all inevitably go through. We all will feel the loss of someone we love. We must realize that we will survive.

Even though it might not be clear right now, your light on this earth is needed. There is no one else on earth like you because you are indeed unique. People need you! At a time of loss, you may experience a sense of self-imposed guilt or worthlessness, thinking *if only* or *I should have*, but this self-abuse is not necessary. Don't feed into it! Realize that the grief you experience can assist you in being a bit more sensitive to others in a similar position. One day you will be able to help someone else go through the grieving process. The loss you suffer, no matter how great, does not compare to the greatness that is you. Be kind to yourself and give yourself a big hug. Tell yourself how much you love and appreciate yourself for being alive and having the strength and courage to go through such an incredible adventure called life!

CHAPTER 10

Making Contact

I have had enormous interest from people who desire to make contact with their departed loved ones on their own. There are others who feel they, too, possess a strong psychic or mediumistic link, and they want to develop this part of themselves further. In this chapter I am providing information for both purposes. It would not be right of me to instruct those of you who just want to make contact with loved ones without providing a basic understanding of the mechanics of mediumship. I believe the more knowledge you have of this material, the more successful the results. I urge you to read over the following concepts and apply them wherever necessary.

This is not a game. It is not my intention to teach you some *tricks* so you can amuse others with your psychic abilities. The development of your intuition must be taken seriously and with respect. You cannot ring a bell and expect a spirit to suddenly appear. In order to be successful, you will have to work at it. Remember, your results will reflect the amount of discipline, time, and desire you have to develop your abilities. At the same time, you must realize that your spirit family also shares a desire to get in contact with you and would do anything possible to let you know that they are alive.

Spirits are constantly around us, and although some are able to get through without much work on our part, others may find it quite difficult. We are all mediums in our own right. As we have become aware, a medium is an instrument, an *in-between*, that the spirit world utilizes to convey a particular message. For what is mediumship but being inspired with thoughts, words, or feelings different from our own? Artists, musicians, doctors, chefs, and almost every living creature is inspired by thoughts. Many times we may think these thoughts are our own, but more often than not, they emanate from spiritual realms. Through these thoughts, the best parts of our creative character come forth. Creativity is not limited to the arts. A doctor utilizing a scalpel is just as creative in his science as a ballerina performing a pirouette.

When we think of making contact with the spiritual realms, we first must approach it with the awareness that the spirit world, or the creative sense of God, is not limited to an area in the clouds out of our reach. Rather, this creative spirit is up, down, around, and through us. It is intermingled within our own world. We must realize that this physical world is just one dimension of many, that our solar system is but one of many, and that the being known as human is just one species of many. Our first lesson, then, is to possess a totally open mind and enter this work with a sense of humility and love. When we open ourselves up to the spiritual realms, we must enter into the work with as much knowledge as is available. The more aware and certain we are of the techniques, the etiquette involved, and the natural spiritual laws, the more effective the mediumship can be, and the clearer and more precise are the results.

When I first started my own journey, I read over one hundred books originating from various parts of the world. The books I scanned included those written fifty years or so ago to those of the present day. I spoke to as many psychics, mediums, and spiritual teachers as I could find. I visited many nondenominational churches in my area. Of course, my interests were to pursue this work to help humankind and to spread the love and knowledge of life after death. If you just want to be able to contact loved ones or guides, your motivation is quite different from mine. You do not have to go through the extent of homework that I did, but remember, the more aware you are of this work, the easier it will be to understand and accomplish certain results.

Discipline plays a very intricate part in developing any spiritual gifts or spiritual communication. Although you have a desire to reach your spirit family, it does not mean that you can turn off the lights and they magically appear. You must do this work in a disciplined, serious state. Anything done in a haphazard manner can be dangerous, and results can be anything but satisfying. Once again, if you want to make contact or open up to the spiritual worlds, I urge you do so, not out of a sense of amusement or curiosity, but with a sense of reverence, humility, discipline, and respect. Your spiritual evolvement is not a cheap trick or a crazy amusement. Like attracts like, and you will get out of your work what you put into it. Therefore, venture into this work with an understanding of the applicable physical and spiritual laws that govern it. In order to start, you must have a grasp of basic spiritual and physical laws and how they apply to your development.

Motivation and Desire

What is the reason behind your interest in developing your inner abilities and contacting your loved ones? Is it something frivolous like asking for the winning lottery numbers? Is it to find out where a relative left the will so you can get your share of the estate? Is it to find out the name of the person who murdered your child? Or is it one of idle curiosity? If your interest pertains to any one of these reasons, then my best advice would be to read a good mystery or suspense novel and obtain your excitement from that. You cannot seek contact in order to get revenge or to satisfy personal greed. There is no room for self-indulgence in spirit; it is only the work of selfless love. For love is the strongest component in bringing us closer to spirit. If you want to make contact and explore the spiritual realms, and by doing so advance yourself spiritually and in turn enlighten others, then and only then would I agree that your motivations are correct.

Preparation

Whenever we do psychic work, we must prepare ourselves accordingly in order to be a clear channel for spirit. Preparation takes place not only on the physical level but on the emotional, mental, and spiritual levels as well.

Physically, one should eat a sound diet. The purer the diet, consisting mostly of vegetarian cuisine, with very little or no refined sugars and caffeine, the better the body can channel spirit. Red meat, in particular, slows down the vibration of the body and in doing so slows down one's higher ranges of sensitivity. The number one glandular system used in this work is our endocrine glands, and specifically, the adrenals. Therefore, we must protect them and put as little stress upon them as possible. Sweets and caffeine, aside from playing havoc with our blood sugar levels, also have an adverse affect on the adrenal system by speeding it up. Alcohol lowers the body's natural vibratory rate and should never be used when one is preparing to open oneself up to the spiritual worlds. The continued use of alcohol, and drugs as well, could very possibly draw entities to you who are on lower vibratory rates of the astral world. These entities could easily influence you and the information you are receiving in a negative or detrimental way. Remember, you are opening yourself to many levels of spirit. You want to make sure to do everything possible to link up to the highest one possible.

Your emotional and mental states need preparation as well. It is necessary to keep your mental and emotional life well balanced when doing this work. Your mental thoughts are real, and they have a direct result on how you feel. Therefore, always try as best you can to keep a positive outlook on life. To do this, I highly rec-

ommend some sort of meditation, visualization, or positive affir-
mation in the morning when waking up. Remember, many of your
first thoughts affect how you will live the rest of your day.

The emotions work hand in hand with your nervous system. If
your nervous system is disturbed and stressed, it can shut down
important channels of psychic energy that travel up and down the
spinal area of the etheric body. You cannot receive clean and refined spiritual information when these centers are blocked. It is
very interesting to note that whenever I do readings and a spirit
comes through crying because it is excited to speak to its loved
one, I find that my receiving centers or channels are blocked because of the spirit's emotional state. Every system works in uni-
son, and one is not more important than another. You want to
make sure you are a well-balanced individual.

Another vital element is the preparation of the spiritual self.
Our spiritual work is one of service and love. We must always as-
pire to bring as much love and understanding to everyone with
whom we come in contact. Our spirit friends and guides want to
work with us. We want to make sure that we give them an instrument worth their time. The spirit people more than anything love
to bestow their knowledge of higher worlds upon us. They are always searching for someone to bring through the message of love
to every part of the planet, but spirit can only bring information
that is within the comprehension of the medium. For instance, if I
were asked to play a Brahms piano concerto in F minor and I
have no knowledge of music, it would be impossible for me to
play because it is out of my experience. If, on the other hand, I
took piano lessons for years and had an understanding of music,
playing Brahms may be elementary to me. Therefore, in order to
bring through knowledge of the highest caliber from the heaven
worlds, one should constantly attune oneself to the highest of
spiritual properties, the highest being love.

Begin to live a life of love and service in all you encounter and
all you do. Be a living example of the precept of love. See all things
as an expression of that creative love called God. Know that there
is no need for judgment, for judgment is of the lower physical self,

or ego, and what right do you have to judge others because they haven't learned a certain human lesson yet? Judgment often stems from fear. Fear is not living in the Godself. Rather, fear prompts you to turn your back on the truth. In striving for a higher understanding of the expression of self, you need to put away that which is not real: judgments, prejudices, and petty ego stroking. Instead, open yourself to the light of tolerance and love—love in its purest form—and don't attempt to cloud the picture with unnecessary trivialities.

When we attempt to develop our spiritual selves, we should strive to learn through reading spiritual literature, meditation, and the like. I find it is also quite an educational and humbling lesson to walk down the street and experience the living conditions of our planet and psychically spread light and love to those who have lost their way and need guidance.

Sensitivity and Awareness

When we deal with the spiritual realms, we are dealing with a world very different from anything we can see with our physical eyes. To do this work properly, we must begin to turn off the outside world and be prepared to enter into a world of inner sight and knowledge. In every class I teach, I begin my lecture by informing people that we are going on an exploration to a new world, a new universe all its own, the world of our inner being. This world is available to anyone who is willing to take the time to become aware of it. By exploring and opening up to our inner self, we bring a new awareness into every aspect of our lives. We begin to really *live* a more fulfilled existence than ever imagined, and a happier life—the kind we dream of. At the center of this world, we greet our Godself, and we behold the limitless possibilities that are a part of our makeup. As we become comfortable in utilizing this *inner knowingness*, we begin to learn how to replace fear with trust in every situation in our lives. Once we have moved into this part of the journey, we can never look at the physical world in the way we once did. It is very difficult to go back to the way we once perceived life.

To become aware of your inner world, it is best to start with a meditation. The first step is to close your eyes and become conscious of your breathing. As you do, you will realize that each inhalation is a gift from God and should be treated properly with a sense of reverence and respect. You never know when your last one will be. As you exhale, see all the unnecessary thoughts and negative feelings, frustrations, and doubts you hold on to, and let them go. Become aware of your body! Sense every muscle, organ, and tissue. See your blood flowing freely throughout your body. Feel! God gave you a body, not only to sustain life on this physical planet, but to evolve from within, so you can become the highest spiritual being possible. So, become aware of everything! When you open your eyes, don't just see the chair in front of you, or the door, or flowers. See them with new eyes—eyes of the soul, the inner eyes. Use your eyes as you do your hands. Feel the life force of the flowers and the trees. Become attuned to the vibration of energy in every living creature. These energies are very real, but they are not overtly obvious. They are subtle energies that you can sense only through your feelings.

Energy

Everything is made of *energy*! We must familiarize ourselves with this understanding. Molecules of a life force surround us and run through us all the time. Therefore, we are each an individual energy center, a little world of our own with energy circles and links running in and around our body. We can change these energy patterns, colors, and frequencies based upon our thoughts and desires. We can send out energy and receive energy as long as our channels are open and sensitized.

How can we feel this energy?

Let's start with a simple exercise that will introduce you to this energy. Close your eyes and hold your palms facing each other about two feet apart. Hold them there for about three to four seconds. Place all your awareness to the area between the palms and very slowly move them together as though you were squeezing an accordion. Sense the feeling between the palms as they move closer together. Move your hands in a circular motion and feel the subtle energy shifts. You might have to try this a couple of times, but don't worry, you will feel it eventually. You can hold your hand about three inches above any body part and slowly move your palm toward it. The more you do this, the more you will become aware of the subtleties of energy surrounding the body. You might notice that certain parts of the body seem denser than others. Some parts of the body may seem to have more energy for a number of reasons. One could be a remnant from an old injury. Whenever an injury occurs in the body, it not only affects the physical body but the etheric body as well. Therefore, there is usually some sort of indication of an injury, most commonly more concentrated energy. Another reason energy is concentrated in a certain part of the body might be a health condition. As mentioned above, a prevailing health condition registers in the etheric body, and the energy around it is usually denser in appearance and seems to be a different color than the rest of the aura.

Energy Centers

When developing your psychic abilities it is important to educate yourself with the seven main energy centers. These energy centers are known as chakras, a Sanskrit word meaning "wheel of energy." These seven main chakras are positioned on the border of the etheric body and are the doorway or gateway to your etheric energies. The etheric body, or etheric double as it is sometimes called, is the energy body that surrounds the physical body. It is an exact replica of the physical. The etheric body is the one closest to the physical state. Each chakra of the etheric body is different in appearance and color and vibrates or spins at its own particular speed and sends energy—spiritual, mental, emotional, or physical—to its corresponding level.

Root Chakra

This is located at the base of the spine and is known as the seat of our life force. On the physical level, it is associated with the spine, adrenals, kidneys, and colon. It is a red energy and represents our survival instinct—a strong physical capacity and vitality. It is used to ground our energies back into our body. It is also used to draw up cosmic energies from the earth in order to vitalize other chakra centers.

Solar Plexus Chakra

Known also as the sacral chakra, this center is located two inches below the navel. It is the seat of all intuition and psychic sensitivity. It is known as a *feeling center*—a place where all raw emotions are stored. Because this center is primarily on a feeling level, clairsentience and psychometry emanate from this area. On a physical level, it is associated with the sexual organs, spleen, and the bladder. It corresponds with the color of orange.

Spleen Chakra

This third center is located above the navel in the spleen area. At this level, raw emotions are elevated to a finer vibration. This is the center of our feelings, will, and autonomy. This area affects the digestion and the organs of the stomach, pancreas, adrenals, liver, and gall bladder. On the physical level, it is the connection to the *silver cord* and enables us to astral-travel. The silver cord is a concentration of energy in the form of a tether that connects the etheric body to the physical body. It is seen clairvoyantly as a silvery white color. At night when we sleep, we leave the physical body and travel for miles in the astral world. We are able to do this because our etheric body, the one that travels, is connected to our physical body by this lifeline or cord. At the time of actual physical death, the silver cord snaps, and the etheric body is freed. The spleen chakra usually appears as the color yellow.

Heart Chakra

Located in the center of the chest, between the shoulder blades, the heart chakra is the seat of unconditional love. Here the higher spiritual elements of compassion, trust, giving, receiving, and nurturing are felt, and the desire to serve people. It is associated with trance work and feeling the presence of spirit beings. Physically, it is associated with the heart, thymus gland, and circulation system. Green is the color of this center.

Throat Chakra

When this center is developed, it is used for clairaudience—to hear spirit. One actually can hear a physical-sounding voice of the spirit being, or may hear thoughts as if listening to the spirit. It also works with the heart center for trance work. In mediumship, the throat chakra, along with the spleen and solar plexus chakras, assists with direct voice mediumship or channeling. This center is the source of all creative expression. In the physical body, it directly affects the thyroid, hypothalamus, throat, and mouth. Meditate to the color of blue when opening this center.

Third Eye Chakra

Probably the chakra area most known to the public, this very important center is located in the center of the forehead. When developed on a psychic level, it is used for the gift of clairvoyance. When opened, we can see auras, images of all shapes and colors, and spirit people. In the physical body, it is associated with the ears, the pituitary gland, the pineal gland, and the nose. The color indigo corresponds to this seat of vision.

Crown Chakra

The seventh center is located at the very top of the head. This center is the doorway to the higher or cosmic forces. When developed, it can be used to influence all the other centers and bring the highest of spiritual truths to all *sensitive work*. It is the seat of prayer and protection, mysticism and enlightenment. Meditate on a beautiful violet color, which represents this chakra. It influences the cerebral cortex and central nervous system of the physical body.

Patience

To grow from our experiences, we must give ourselves the proper amount of time to develop, for everything has a rhythm and creative energy all its own. In many cases, especially in the paranormal, there is no clock to measure our progress. One of the most important tools is patience. We begin to give birth to a new side of ourselves—a part that has been dormant for many, many years. The past years have been filled with various belief systems, behaviors, and emotionally charged experiences, and we must dig through them in order to bring ourselves back to the truth and our infinite source. I am speaking of that child part that we closed down at the age of six or seven when innocence was replaced with rational thought. In this work, the more we use the rational mind, the less progress we will make. When we expend too much energy analyzing a thought or message, we leave little of that precious energy to utilize for the actual psychic and spiritual work. Progress takes time.

With patience and discipline, you will see changes. Be kind to yourself and enjoy every bit of sensitivity of which you are becoming aware. Enjoy the excitement. Do not be put off if the results do not happen right away. Your spirit guides and friends know you are trying, and they, too, will do their best to work with what is given to them. Remember, you come into this work with old mind-sets, and it takes time for spirit to remold your mind and awaken your sensitivity. Be patient!

An Open Mind

When you enter the world of spirit, you enter a world that most people don't believe exists. Most people have shut down their feelings years ago in the hope that such numbing would help them to survive the emotional turmoil of the physical world.

Every day we experience things that cannot be explained. Some refer to these experiences as coincidences, accidents, or sheer luck. *There is no such thing!* When we are true to ourselves and send out thoughts of our needs and desires, often what we persist in thinking comes into our lives. We bring those experiences that help us to learn and grow. I tell clients during our readings to release all preconceived ideas or expectations about what will happen. In that way, they can be ready for all possibilities. With an open mind, we can gain insight into ideas and expressions that we may have overlooked or not noticed at all.

Cooperation

You are not doing this work alone. You are in partnership with those in the spirit world. As I have stated, you do your part, and spirit does its part. When you want to contact the spirit world, you have to realize that spirit people have free will. If they choose to come in, they will work with the energy vibrations and concentrate on giving you a message. But they may also not wish to. If they choose to work with you, they must understand what you are trying to communicate. Even though they have passed over, it does not mean they immediately know the mechanics of spirit communication. You have to let them know *how* you want them to communicate. Tell them to impress you in a certain way. For instance, if you want to know if it is a female or male energy coming through, ask them to impress you with their gender. Secondly, if you want to know whether you are speaking to a mother or a father, you need to set up a system of communication and explain how it works so spirit people can accommodate you.

This is an example of how I work. If I am communicating with a father or someone from the father's family, I invite the spirit to stand on the left side of the individual. If the spirit is from the mother's side, I tell it to stay on the right side of the person for whom I am reading. If the spirit is a child, I ask it to stand in front of the person, and if it is a grandparent, to stand behind the sitter. In this way, there is a clear system for the spirit people to use.

Also, if you are not hearing them, you need to send them a thought mentally to *make it louder*. Spirit is not always aware of the various frequencies to which they have to adjust in order to be heard. *You* must tell them.

Often, people will see me turning my head and speaking to the empty air: *Yes, I heard that; No, speak up*. This is my way of informing spirit about our communication. So, you see, you need to set up your own rules based on cooperation and trust.

How often should I contact the spirits? Will I disturb them? Many have asked me these questions, and I can only reiterate what I have mentioned earlier. Your family and friends who have passed into another state of consciousness do not forget you. They are more accessible to you in this state than they were living on the earth. They know more about your soul's path and motivation than while they were alive. They come into your vibration and check on you very often. At the same time, even though a spirit is beckoned, it does not mean that it will drop everything to make contact with you. Spirits have free will and will use it accordingly, the same as they did on the earth.

Just as you go to work every day and fulfill a job in order to sustain your life here on this planet, when your family or friends pass into the world of spirit, they also fill their existence with so-called jobs and work to progress themselves spiritually. When you call on them with your thoughts, they hear you *loud and clear*. So, if you call them all the time, it is the same as your sitting at your desk when the phone keeps ringing. It would be difficult to get your work done. Of course, you can call on them from time to time, and this is expected, but do not become obsessed with it, for you are not only holding them back from their progress but keeping yourself from the work you need to accomplish here.

Love

You are on this earth to learn basic lessons of love and responsibility of self and others. These lessons present themselves in our everyday experiences. Anytime you begin to work with spirit, you must come from a center place of love. There should be no greed or need for self-importance. Spiritual work allows no room for the ego. I am not saying that to be a spiritual person, you must be void of ego. Ego is important in order to get the work done. But one must never let the ego go before the love. As you develop, you will begin to see the many different and varying aspects of love, for there are many forms of love. The more you become involved with this work, the more you will begin to recognize even the smallest act of love as significant.

Development Exercises

Meditation

To increase your sensitivity and inner awareness of the spiritual realms, you should begin a regular practice of meditation. Your desire to develop will determine the length of time spent in meditation. If you are just starting out, I would recommend meditation at least twice a week. Make it a habit to meditate at the same time on the appointed day. In this way you not only begin to set up a sense of discipline but also let the spirit world know that it is your time for spiritual practice and development. The length of time of meditation varies. If you can, try to sit for at least fifteen minutes the first time, slowly working up to thirty minutes and gradually to forty-five minutes. However, do not feel pressured about how much time you spend. The amount of time will eventually be guided by spirit, not by you.

In the next chapter I have included a detailed description of various meditations that you can use. There is no right or wrong way to meditate. The idea behind this exercise is to make sure you are in a state of relaxation. You are striving to get in touch with the inner worlds and become more sensitized to them.

Circle

Most people who are interested in pursuing their mediumistic gifts usually find it much more beneficial and more expeditious, in addition to meditating on their own, to sit in what is known as a development circle. A development circle is made up of two or more individuals who come together each week at the same time to sit and develop the mediumistic energies of the participants in the circle.

Usually a circle consists of the same participants who sit at the same time each week. It is important that the group members are harmonious to each other's energies. There should be no conflict or ego problems. Otherwise, such conflict will have a negative result on the group's development and hinder the group from attaining the highest of spiritual teachings available to them. You will always draw those spirit beings to your group who work well with the vibration created. Being a group member is a commitment and should not be entered unless all are willing to sacrifice at least one to two hours the same time each week. The reason is quite simple: To perfect and sensitize a member or several members of the group, the spirit world sets aside a time to attune themselves to the group's energies to assist in building up these energies. The idea is to build upon the basic foundation work each week, not to constantly redo what has been done.

When a circle is created, one person should be picked to lead the group. This is usually someone who has a certain amount of experience with psychic development. At the opening of the circle, a prayer should be said to welcome spirit guides and friends who are present to work with you and to ask for their assistance in protecting the group. At the end of the prayer, I ask all of the participants to envision a white light of love around the circle and throughout the room for an added dose of protection.

After the prayer, the group may want to listen to spiritual or uplifting music as an added source of energy. Spirit, too, makes use of this kind of music. At this point, some groups open the floor to discussion. I suggest that you keep speaking to a minimum, since this takes away from the time the spirits can help in development work.

Prior to the onset of the development circle, all participants should decide to whom in the group the energy is to be directed. Maybe only one is mediumistic, and the group may want to work together in developing that person's sensitivities further. Where several members are mediumistic, it is important to direct the energies evenly throughout. This is where the leader comes in. He or she should keep track of time and let the group know when to move on to another member. The idea is to focus all mental energy to that person in the color of white, the color that represents the Christ light of love.

As you sit in the circle, you may begin to feel a sense of coolness around the lower parts of your body. This is usually spirits attuning themselves to the energies in the room. You may also begin to see trivial signs and symbols in your third eye. These images may rush into your consciousness as various shapes like circles or squares, colored lights, scenes, objects, faces, and random forms in space. Many times these images are equivalent to the scenes or objects seen during dreams. Do not regard them as mere nonsense, as they may mean something to someone else in the group. As best you can, try to remember all that you see, feel, and hear. Even though you may not be able to interpret the information, you may be very surprised to see how much of your information is significant to another member. Eventually, someone in the group may begin to sense a strange feeling around the head or chest area. To me, it feels like cobwebs. Again, this means that spirit directors are working with your energies. Mostly it is an ectoplasmic aura around you. This ectoplasm develops more and more each time the group gets together. It is usually prevalent when someone in the group has physical mediumship gifts. The spirits build up this energy around that individual, and often others might begin to hear *raps* or *knocks* as spirits test out the individual's energy.

When it is time for the circle to conclude, the leader informs all to slowly come back into awareness of their physical bodies. When everyone is safely back—and it is important to wait until they are all back—then the leader says a closing prayer, thanking all the spirit helpers. I usually like to send out love and light to those less fortunate in the world. When the prayer is completed, it is time for everyone in the group to share with the other members. Any sensations, messages, or signs received during the circle should be reviewed.

Basic Psychic Exercises

Success in the spirit world is measured by an individual's sensitivity. Work either with meditation or in a circle. Both will prepare you to feel and perhaps see and hear spirit.

The time comes when you are ready to put into practice your psychic and spiritual abilities. As I have stated throughout this book, everything is energy. After your preparation, you can begin to utilize this energy and learn what you can feel from it. The following are ways to test your skills.

Psychometry

Psychometry is an ability to feel or sense the history of an object or the person to whom it belongs through the emanations of energy from the object. Psychometry can be used with someone who has passed over to the other side or for anyone still living on the physical plane. First, of course, get into a meditative or light trance state in which you are totally relaxed. Next, hold an object with your left hand and immediately sense the energy of the object. You may receive impressions such as physical characteristics or the appearance of the bearer of the object. You may receive feelings on an emotional basis. Remember, psychometry can be done with any object, including photographs. Through the exercise of psychometry you can get not only impressions from those living but messages from the spirit world. Again, do not think of what you are getting, and *don't* hold on to the thought. Express exactly what you are receiving.

Automatic Writing

Automatic writing is an exercise used specifically for those who desire to contact spirit guides and loved ones. It requires a complete meditative state to begin. It is also necessary to send out a thought to the spirit to be contacted with the exact time and place that will be used to do this work. In essence, you are making an appointment to talk to the spirit world. When the appointed time arrives, become meditative. Remember, you want to be in a room where there are few or no distractions. Next, sit upright at a table with a pad of paper and pen in front of you. Lightly hold a pen to the pad. *Do not think* of what to write. When you feel a change in the energy in your hand or around your body, begin to ask questions of the spirit. Most likely, you will feel an urgency to begin writing, so go with it. Again, *do not think* of what you are writing. It is a good idea not to look at it until you are finished. When you sense the energy has left, put down the pen and read what your spirit friend has stated. You may be surprised at what you receive.

Dreams

Many people have asked if it is possible to reach those who have passed over through dreams. The answer is an unequivocal YES! The spirit body leaves the physical body every night when we go to sleep. The physical body is replenished with cosmic energies, and the spirit body is doing the same on a higher level. In the dream state we are very susceptible to impressions from spirit because we are not involved on a conscious or mental level. In other words, much of our control is at rest, as is our rational thinking. Therefore, we can be more easily impressed. In the spirit body we are able to see our loved ones and guides and possibly foresee future events or even past lives. It is also a time when our spirit family communicates with us. Since we are closer to the spirit levels in our dream state, it is much easier to communicate with those who have passed on. As I said in a previous chapter, the easiest way to reach spirits in the sleep state is to think about them before falling asleep. Many of my clients have used this method with success. However, many of us do not remember our visits, or we might recall just glimpses or pieces. Usually, our dreams don't make sense at all. Remembering dreams takes practice and discipline.

There are several ways to remember your dreams. One is to keep a tape recorder by your bed, and as soon as you awaken, record any impressions, scenes, and feelings from your dreams. You can also write them down, but most people find this method harder to continue over a period of time. If you get in the habit of recording your dreams, you will be amazed by how much more you are likely to remember them.

Visions

Many have said that they see their loved one standing in their room next to the bed or sitting in the living room chair. When you are more receptive and not mentally blocked, it is very possible for you to indeed see them.

Make a Pact

Another exercise to contact the spirit world is simply to ask your spirit friend to be present at a particular time of the day. Explain that you want proof of their existence by their doing a particular task. For instance, a client whose son passed over asked him every night: *I want you to set up a signal with me that you are here. Blink on the streetlamp once if your answer is yes and twice if your answer is no.* After two months of this daily request, she found he was responding exactly the way she asked. This may not be successful for everyone who attempts it. Obviously, this mother and her spirit son were quite determined, and the results were successful. It is easier when you ask the spirits to demonstrate their presence by performing little tasks. Don't ask them to move objects, or open doors, or sing a song. MAKE IT EASY! Due to the energy makeup of spirits, we have found the easiest way for them to make themselves known is to use something electrical. Spirits can affect electricity in a variety of ways. Many spirit people are able to influence the electrical force field of protons and electrons and effect changes in various electrical objects throughout the house. This is usually most prevalent if the deceased was someone of a very high emotional caliber. Emotional energy can be used as a conductor.

Results

The following are ways spirits let their loved ones know that they are around them without the use of a medium:

- **Lights.** Many times you will see the flickering of lights in the room, or new lightbulbs burn out instantly. More often than not, your lights are affected when the spirit spends a lot of time around you or when they know it is a way to get your attention.
- **Television.** Spirits have been known to effectively scramble pictures on the TV set. There have been cases when the spirit's face has appeared on the screen or the television turns on and off by itself at strange hours or odd times of the day.
- **Radios.** Many clock radios next to loved ones' beds will turn on at different hours. Sometimes it is an hour that has some sort of significance to the loved one who passed. Many times the radio will go on when a particularly significant song is on the air.
- **Music.** Many times in their own way, spirits are able to impress you with a song, or you may think about them when a song is played on the radio.
- **Clocks.** It has been reported that a clock will stop at the exact moment the loved one passed over, or a clock or watch will stop working for no obvious reason.
- **Telephones and Answering Machines.** After someone dies, it is possible to receive a phone call and no one is on the other end of the line. Or you may actually hear the voice of the spirit.

In some cases the voice has been recorded on answering machines.

- **Appliances.** Appliances have been known to stop or start working at different times when no one is around them. It is another way that spirits attempt to get our attention. I have found this quite common, especially if a spirit was very involved with cooking or spent much of its time in the kitchen area while alive.

- **Computers.** EVP, or Electronic Voice Phenomenon, has become quite a popular result in the past several months. Not only has the spirit world been able to utilize telephones and answering machines, but spirits have also appeared on the screens of computers. There is no rhyme or reason for this activity, other than a spirit who wants to reassure a loved one that it is indeed alive. A spirit might also have had an interest in computers as well.

Other Signs

- **Smells.** A very common sign immediately after or within several months following a transition is scent. Suddenly, one becomes aware of a faint smell of a cigar, or roses, or a familiar perfume. These scents are definitely associated with those who have departed. For instance, a person's mother might have used a particular perfume, and unexpectedly it pervades the room. The same goes for cigarette odor if a loved one was a smoker. These scents and odors are ways loved ones let us know they are nearby.

- **Gifts.** Spirit sends many gifts and material items, but we do not connect that they are from our loved ones. Many times I have done readings and a loved one will come through and say, "I hope you like the gold necklace I bought you last week?" The client will look up at me dumbfounded and ask, "What are you talking about?" I explain that spirit can impress us to buy certain things. Some of the ways spirits intervene for us are, for example, when we receive a dozen roses out of the blue, or if we buy a house and have little problem closing the sale, or if we suddenly get a job that we wanted. These are signs that our loved ones are with us and want to assist us.

- **Animals.** Animals are often used by spirit. Many times spirit beings can influence a bird or small animal to come by us to get our attention in some way. It is another sign of their nearness to us. A good friend of mine died in February. I went to New York, which was buried under two feet of snow, to visit her outdoor crypt. I had trouble locating it when suddenly a truck pulled up, and a groundskeeper stepped out. "You're staring right at it," he said. I thanked him, and he went back to his truck and drove away. I thought it strange that he just happened to come by at that very moment. After he left, I looked up to her niche and next to it, a bright blue jay perched itself on the branch of a tree. Mind you, it was very cold with snow everywhere. I didn't think it so unusual until later that afternoon when I visited her husband, Jack, at their home. I walked in the door, and Jack's first words were, "If you want anything of Connie's, please take it." I turned my head to the right, and there on a shelf was a glass bluebird staring back at me.

CHAPTER 11

Meditations

It gives one solace to know that in a cold, disheartening world, where tragedy and intolerance appear to dominate, and the reasonable and rational self is nothing but a dream, a refuge exists where love stands supreme. It is a world of unlimited potential intermingled with divine bliss. This world of delight is available to everyone who chooses to open that door. Where is this place of contentment and love? This domain of peace is found in SILENCE. It is the silence of *being* . . . just being. For it is in the golden silence of our own selves that the divine is found.

When we center ourselves and listen to that still small voice within, we are tapping into the silence of being. This *self-knowingness* can be utilized in every aspect of life to ripen and enrich every experience. So many people go through their daily lives in search of their purpose for living. They bemoan their fate and suffer so. If they would just take a simple moment to stop and listen to their inner voice, they would begin to open themselves up to a level of indefatigable understanding. But how do we get to this SILENCE? How do we tap into our inner knowingness? How do we discern our inner voice? The answer to these questions, and the best way I know, is through meditation.

What is meditation? Simply, meditation is a focus of consciousness from one state of being to another. In essence, we turn off the outside, everyday world and tune in to, or become aware of, our inside world. When we sit in silence and begin to focus our attention inwardly, the awareness of self is strengthened and the spiritual dimensions of the soul are revealed. When we meditate or concentrate our energies on our *beingness*, we return to wholeness, the oneness of who we are—our infinite self. In that oneness, we begin to discard the idea of duality that separates us from our Godself. This duality is based on the falsehood of negativity, fear, anxiety, illness, grief, and disappointment, all of which become our reality when we are not in tune with our divine self.

As we meditate, we utilize cosmic energies, and they, in turn, illuminate and energize the various spirit centers of the body. This energy is focused primarily in our heart chakra or center. When we meditate, the light of unconditional love is lit within us, and it continues to grow more and more with each meditation. We must remember that the heart center is the embodiment of the Christ Consciousness, or the seat of the soul. The more we focus on this center, the more our feelings of unconditional love evolve, and, in turn, the more we transform every aspect of our lives and influence everyone with whom we come in contact. All things start in the heart center. As we meditate, our psychic centers are heightened because the stream of the Christ Consciousness that originates in the heart center flows through all the psychic centers, or chakras, of the body. We eventually tune in to this energy or stream of light as it flows throughout the body.

How to Meditate

When people hear the word *meditation*, their first impression is one of a yogi in a lotus position who chants "Oms" in a room filled with incense. Some of this is true. We can sit in a lotus position and chant "Om," but we don't have to. Meditation is merely a concentrated focus. The more we practice it, the more we are able to get in the flow of an infinite life force.

At the same time, many other forms of meditation do not require absolute stillness of body. The one I will be discussing further in this chapter is a formal way to meditate, but meditation can be done in many ways. For example, this same kind of focus of energy can also be accomplished while we paint, garden, write, sing, act, dance, work, exercise, drive, and so on. Whenever we tune in to the creative force within ourselves, we are, in essence, meditating.

Preliminaries

The following suggestions can be used at the beginning of any meditation or relaxation exercise. I call these *preliminaries*.

1. Setting Aside a Place for Meditation
The first thing to do is to pick a room in your home for your practice of meditation. It can be a bedroom, living room, or guest room. Remember, this room is to be used for your spiritual exercises, so you might think of it as a spiritual workroom. The important thing to keep in mind is that this is a place reserved for relaxation and inner work. You may set aside an area of the room where you can meditate without interruption, where there is very little or no interference from the outside world.

Before you begin, turn off all phones, answering machines, and beepers. Turn off anything that could be distracting or disturbing. If you like, you can light some incense or place a vase of fresh flowers in the room. You can play a tape of soft and relaxing music, but nothing that is jarring or loud. These are some tools that can assist your inward focus.

2. Choosing a Meditative Position
You may choose to sit on the floor, if that is comfortable, or in a flat-back chair, which I find more comfortable. No matter what

your choice is, it is important that your spine be erect as though you are being pulled by a string from the top of the head. In this manner, the energies are able to flow more easily up and down the spine.

If you are sitting in a chair, your legs should be uncrossed and flat on the floor, and your palms should face upwards resting on your thighs. If you sit on the floor, bend your legs in a yoga position with your feet facing each other, knees on the floor, and your palms facing upwards on your thighs.

3. Relaxation Exercise

Once in position, concentrate on your breathing. This is a vital element in meditation. When you first start out, you may find it takes effort and timing to get into the rhythm of your breathing. This is true with anything, but even more so with meditation. After some practice, you won't even notice the breath; it will automatically rise and fall into place naturally in its proper manner. The key is slow, relaxed, deep breathing from your midsection, not shallow, quick breaths.

When you begin to breathe, close your eyes. Think of your breath as everything, for without it, you are not able to live. Begin the inhalation slowly through the nose. As you do this, envision a golden, white light, representing the *Christ light*, about two inches above your head. Inhale this light through your entire being; see it enter the head area, travel through the throat and chest into the arms and hands, then descend down the rest of the torso, legs, and feet. Hold the breath for a count of four and see its golden color fill every cell of the body with a sense of unconditional love, purity, and wholeness. At the end of four, exhale the breath out of the mouth. As you exhale, imagine any negativity, stress, or anxiety that has been pent up in the body slowly leave through the mouth as a gray mist. With each exhalation, you will feel lighter as you free yourself of heavy and denser energies. These heavier energies will be replaced with the lighter and higher vibrations of the Christ golden light.

As you become more relaxed, envision each body part, and release any stress held inside of the body part. You can do this by tightening the area and then relaxing it, thereby letting go of stress. With your mind's eye, envision your toes, tighten them, and then release them. Do the same with your ankles, calves, and thighs. Move to the buttocks, the pelvic area, then the stomach, midsection, and chest area. You want to fully relax the back, the neck, the shoulders, and all of the head area. Finally, tighten then relax the arms, including the biceps and triceps, and the hands. Make a fist with each hand, then release it. Remember to bring the golden light to every area of your body as you tighten and relax it.

After this exercise, you should be fully relaxed and ready for meditation. In such a relaxed state, it is easier to focus your energies on the meditation exercise. Listed below are three exercises that I have included for your use. If, however, you just want a quick way of relaxing from a day's stress, you can do the relaxation exercise by itself.

Saying Good-bye to Loved Ones and Sending Them on Their Way

After you have completed the preliminaries, you can use this exercise to release your loved one into spirit. Begin by picturing your loved one in your mind's eye. See him as the picture of perfect health standing right in front of you. Any illness, whether cancer, AIDS, Alzheimer's, or another, no longer has any bearing on his new body. Even if his was a quick passing of some kind, or even a traumatic one, just picture the person as complete, happy, and full of life, standing in front of you.

Picture as many details as possible. You may see your loved one in a familiar dress or outfit. If you can, imagine her aroma or scent. Perhaps she had a specific birthmark, or a significant stance, or a particular hairdo. The more detailed you are in your visualization, the more successful the exercise.

Once you have a detailed picture of your loved one in mind, begin a conversation. Ask him about his transition to spirit. Ask: *How do you feel now?* Tell him how you have been since his death. Tell him about the grief you still feel. Talk to your loved one, and then listen to the answers back to you. *Do not stop* the exercise even if you think that you are merely talking to yourself. It is important to completely follow through without rationalizing any part of it. Enjoy being together once again. Perhaps it will bring back a memory of a time when you were together on the physical earth and the enjoyment shared in each other's company.

The next step on your journey is to take your loved one's hand and travel together to a beautiful garden that is filled with bright, beautiful, colorful flowers of different shapes and sizes. Smell the fragrance of this incredible garden. Within this wonderfully landscaped garden are splendid statues and magnificent fountains where birds frolic and sing their songs. Hear the sounds of children playing and sharing laughter in the distance. Every element around you is perfect. Enjoy the splendor, peace, and tranquillity of this special place.

As you look far off into the distance, you see massive buildings. Both of you go toward them. As you get closer, you see the glimmering pillars of pearl of an incredible building. This building shimmers in a light rose color. All around this building are other buildings spread perfectly apart. Each building differs slightly in design, and each encompasses a sense of a heavenly world. You walk inside the massive building together and find yourselves inside a huge living room. In the center of this room is a large movie screen. As you look at the screen, the lights dim and a movie begins. It is a movie of the events and experiences you and your loved one once shared. The picture begins when you first meet each other and goes from there. As you watch all the vivid experiences together, feel the emotion that corresponds with the moment. Do this for as long as it takes. Enjoy the times spent together.

When the film is over, you feel a sense of relief and completion. You have experienced a piece of time together, but it is not over yet, for there are more experiences to share at another time. You begin to understand that you and your loved one have spent lifetimes together in the past, and you'll spend lifetimes together in the future. Life goes on, whether here on earth or in heaven.

Afterwards, you leave the building and travel back to the garden. Among the wonderful, incredible vistas of beautiful flowers and greenery stand several beings dressed in white. *Who are they?* you ask. Your loved one says: *They are my teachers. They are helping me to learn more on this side.* You look into their all-knowing eyes and see their compassion. They smile back assuredly, and you know your loved one is where he belongs. He is home, in a place of incredible life and growth. One of the teachers comes over to you and hands you a silver heart on a silver chain. She tells you to open the heart, and you do. She says, *Fill the heart with all the wonderful things you want your loved one to keep with him in his new world.* Your mind is suddenly full, and all of your thoughts spill into the silver heart: everything you always wanted to tell your loved one, every word you thought but never uttered, every feeling, expressed or not; everything you want him to remember. See these thoughts, feelings, and words filling the inside of the silver heart, and as they do, the heart begins to glow. It shines so brightly with your love you can barely look at it. You place the heart around the neck of your loved one so it will be with him always. It is a part of your love that can never die. You hug your loved one, and he says, *I will always be with you.*

The time comes when you must return to earth, for just as your loved one must continue to learn and work where he is, you, too, must continue your work where you are. And so it is. You leave this land of splendor with a sense of real life and the *knowingness* that you will meet again in the garden of heavenly delights when you have completed your lessons on earth. At that time, your loved one will greet you and escort you back home.

Forgiveness and Regrets

Whenever someone passes, the living relatives and friends are often left with a lot of unspoken feelings and regrets. *What if, if I could,* and *if only* seem to be the words that I hear most often. Those alive feel abandoned and incomplete, as though their hearts are broken and they can no longer continue living life. They would feel much better if they could share their feelings with their loved ones one more time. They don't know how to go on with their burdens and guilt. The following meditation is designed to help let go of such regrets.

After your preliminaries, envision yourself standing in front of a cottage in the middle of a beautiful field. The cottage has been created exactly to your liking, including the color, the wood, and so on. Perhaps there is a porch with a rocking chair. Maybe there is a border of lovely roses on the walkway. See the cottage as yours, for it belongs to no one else but you.

As you enter this house, you immediately see a very comfortable living area with a fluffy, overstuffed sofa full of pillows. To one side is a picture window, and the radiant sunshine filters through it. The wallpaper is made of the finest materials. The room is completely filled with every material item you have ever wanted in your life. Make sure all these items are imbued with your feeling. On the far left wall are several photographs of varying shapes and sizes—pictures of all your family members. You see the faces of those who have passed into the world of spirit and those currently alive. Take down the photo of the individual for whom you are grieving. Bring this framed photograph to the wooden desk in the corner of the room. See this desk exactly as you would have it. This is where you do your special work, the work of the heart. Sit down at your desk and set the picture in front of you. Take out a piece of parchment paper from the desk. Pull out a fountain pen and lay it on the paper.

As you study the photo, ask yourself: *What things do I want to be forgiven for?* Pick up the pen and start writing your list on the paper. Perhaps you were too judgmental to your loved one, or perhaps you didn't show enough love. Maybe you felt as though you weren't there when she needed you. Write down any feeling for which you want forgiveness. Next, take another piece of paper and write down all the regrets you have had since your loved one passed into spirit. Write down the words you didn't tell her when she was alive. Maybe you didn't agree on some issues, and they were left unresolved. Maybe you felt as though you could have loved her more. Write down any feeling that you still hold on to and you cannot or are unable to release.

When you have finished the two lists, roll each one up into a scroll. Next, go over to your beautiful window and feel the spring-time breeze that blows through the room. Next to the window, there are two white balloons. Drop each list into a balloon. Blow up the balloon, tie it off, and set it free out the window. Watch as the two balloons slowly dance their way up to heaven. As they soar high in the sky, you feel a sense of lightness as all the regrets leave your being. As the balloons rise higher and higher, you know that they are bound for your loved one in spirit. See your loved one receive the balloons and read the notes. Take a few moments to look out your window at the sky and see a message from your loved one. The message is: *No matter what, I will always love you!*

Rediscovering Your Power

So often in life it is our desire to be loved, and we tend to fall victim to our own making. We try so hard to be the best wife, mother, father, child, employer, lover, or friend. Because we believe it is what is expected in order to have the love of someone else, we compromise who we truly are. For the most part, we do this on an unconscious level, and we are totally unaware of our behavior. After a while, our behavior becomes second nature, and days fall into years as we continually try to live up to their image of us. Eventually, we find ourselves depressed and unhappy about life and unfulfilled in our dreams. At this point, it is difficult to trace back to the *why* and *how* we feel this way. Not only have we given our power and a piece of ourselves to these people, but, more important, we have not been *true to who we are*. We have left our *centeredness* and given away a part of our beautiful self-wholeness. Unfortunately, we can never be truly happy until we live our own lives.

So many people are miserable when their loved ones pass, and much of this pain is the result of compromise—too often, they have given away a part of who they are. They have compromised their individuality; they have not been true to themselves because of the need or desire to please the other. So when loved ones die, they are left with no sense of self-esteem because so much of their identities were tied to the deceased. All that is left is a sense of emptiness and loneliness.

This next meditation is one you can use to regain that part of you that has been lost, taken, or given away. Use this meditation to bring back the creative power that is yours.

Again, begin with the preliminaries. When completed, envision yourself standing in front of a peaceful and serene lake. It is a gentle blue lake that reflects a myriad of magnificent colors of the landscape: rich green, blue, yellow, and violet. You can smell the freshness of the stimulating country air. Two swans swim around the lake and add to the tranquillity of the scene. The more you look at this lake, the more relaxed you become. You take a walk to the far side of the lake and see a stream flowing down a mountain into the lake. You climb up the mountain to locate the origin of this stream. When you reach the top of the mountain, you discover a beautiful cascading waterfall. You look up toward the sky and notice that there is no beginning to the waterfall. It seems to fall right out of the heavens.

You remove your clothes and lay them on a nearby rock. You walk under the waterfall and feel the cool, pristine water caress your body; it is water the likes of which you have never felt. It feels as if feathers are touching your body, and in an instant you feel totally cleansed. You look down at the stream below, and as if looking into a magic mirror, you see all the different circumstances in which you gave away your power. You see the times when you should have been true to yourself. You see how you did not love yourself enough nor treat yourself with respect. As you watch these images, each one slowly floats down the mountain stream.

As you continue to stand under the waterfall, you notice a beautiful light streaming through the falls. As this light touches you, you suddenly feel a rush of energy and a newfound sense of creativity. You begin to feel love running throughout your body. You feel love for yourself, for it is your love that you are finally getting in touch with. As you continue to feel this love and joy, you look into the water, and the images you see are now quite different. You see yourself happy, doing activities you have always wanted to do but never gave yourself the time for. You see people applauding you for how wonderful and loving you are. You see the true you. Feel how much lighter you have become. Feel your strength and potential, once lost, return to you. All that self-assurance resides within you now. You are free of other people's domination. You have taken a wonderful journey to rediscover your true self. Enjoy it.

You leave the waterfall and feel a whole new and wonderful being inside yourself. You are excited about your new self. You look at your clothes. They have been replaced by a beautiful spirit robe. You put on the robe as a reminder that you are invincible. You are truly GOD!

RESOURCES

After We Die, What Then? Answers to Questions About Life After Death by George W. Meek, published by Metascience Corporation, Franklin, North Carolina.

Everyone's Guide to the Hereafter by Ken Akehurst (the blind medium who passed to the Higher Life on July 28, 1978); transmitted through G. M. Roberts, published by Neville Spearman Publishers, C.W. Daniel Company Limited, Essex, England.

Kundalini and the Chakras: A Practical Manual—Evolution in This Lifetime by Genevieve Lewis Paulson, published by Llewellyn Publications, Inc., St. Paul, Minnesota.

Life in the World Unseen by Anthony Borgia, published by M.A.P. Inc., Midway, Utah.

The Mechanics of Mediumship by Ivy Northage, published by Ivy Northage, Emsworth, England.

Opening Up to Your Psychic Self: A Primer on Psychic Development by Petey Stevens, published by Nevertheless Press, Berkeley, California.

The Transition Called Death: A Recurring Experience by Charles Hampton, published by Quest Books, Wheaton, Illinois.

For further information regarding James Van Praagh
send a *self-addressed stamped envelope* to:

Spiritual Horizons, Inc.
7985 Santa Monica Boulevard, Suite 109–135
West Hollywood, California 90046

Or you may contact his website at http://www.VanPraagh.com

· A NOTE ON THE TYPE ·

The typeface used in this book is one of many versions of Garamond, a modern homage to—rather than, strictly speaking, a revival of—the celebrated fonts of Claude Garamond (c. 1480–1561), the first founder to produce type on a large scale. Garamond's type was inspired by Francesco Griffo's *De Ætna* type (cut in the 1490s for Venetian printer Aldus Manutius and revived in the 1920s as Bembo), but its letter forms were cleaner and the fit between pieces of type improved. It therefore gave text a more harmonious overall appearance than its predecessors had, becoming the basis of all romans created on the Continent for the next two hundred years; it was itself still in use through the eighteenth century. Besides the many "Garamonds" in use today, other typefaces derived from his fonts are Granjon and Sabon (despite their being named after other printers).